Air Fryer
Cookbook For Beginners
2020

800 Most Wanted, Quick & Amazingly Easy Recipes to Fry, Bake, Grill, and Roast with Your Air Fryer

Gina Newman

Copyright © 2019 Gina Newman

All rights reserved. No part of this guide may be reproduced in any form without permission in writing from the publisher except in the case of brief quotations embodied in critical articles or reviews.

Legal & Disclaimer

The information contained in this book and its contents is not designed to replace or take the place of any form of medical or professional advice; and is not meant to replace the need for independent medical, financial, legal, or other professional advice or services, as may be required. The content and information in this book have been provided for educational and entertainment purposes only.

The content and information contained in this book have been compiled from sources deemed reliable, and it is accurate to the best of the Author's knowledge, information and However, the Author cannot guarantee its accuracy and validity and cannot be held liable for any errors and/or omissions. Further, changes are periodically made to this book as and when needed.

You agree that by continuing to read this book, where appropriate and/or necessary, you shall consult a professional (including but not limited to your doctor, attorney, or financial advisor or such other advisor as needed) before using any of the suggested remedies, techniques, or information in this book.

CONTENTS

Introduction 7

Chapter 1: Air Fryer Basics 8
   What is air fryer? 8
   Characteristics of air fryers 9
   Benefits of Air Fryer 10
   Tips for using your Air Fryer 11
   Cleaning your Air Fryer 12

Chapter 2: Snacks and Appetizers 13
   Bacon Chicken Roll 13
   Spicy Potato Chips 14
   Crispy Apple And Pear With Oatmeal ... 15
   Buns With Carrots And Nuts 16
   Pine Skewers Aceto Reduction 17
   Mini Burgers 18
   Chicken Sandwich 19
   Potato Balls Stuffed With Ham And Cheese From The Air Fryer 20
   Spring Rolls 21
   Sausages And Chorizos 23
   T-Bone Steak Santa Maria 24
   Steak With Chimichurri 25
   Flank Steak With Balsamic Mustard ... 26
   Italian Meatballs 27
   Japanese Meatballs 28
   Mushroom Croquettes 29
   Sausage Puff Pastry 30
   Peppers Stuffed With Potato Omelette 31
   Longaniza Skewers 32
   Eggplant Milanese 33
   Potato Croquettes 34
   Stuffed Potatoes 35
   Cottage Cheese Spinach Cakes ... 36
   Crispy Tofu 37
   Ripe Bananas Croquettes 38
   Avocado Stuffed With Prawns 39
   Broccoli And Cheese Croquettes ... 40
   Sweet Potato Pie 42

Chapter 3: Breakfast Recipes 43
   Cocotte Eggs 43
   Tortilla 44
   Santa Fe Style Pizza 45
   Grilled Sandwich With Three Types Of Cheese 46
   Sweet Nuts Butter 47
   Zucchini And Walnut Cake With Maple Flavor Icing 48
   Misto Quente 49
   Garlic Bread 50
   Bruschetta 51
   Cream Buns With Strawberries 52
   Blueberry Buns 53
   Cooked Egg In Casserole 54
   French Toast In Sticks 55
   Muffins Sandwich 56
   Streusel Coffee Muffins 57

Bacon BBQ 58

Breakfast Pizza 59

Stuffed French Toast 60

Pepperoni Pizza Bread......................... 61

Curd Cheese With Milanese 62

Cheese Bread 63

Homemade Pizzas 64

Leek Quiche.. 65

Bags Of Mushrooms Grown With Ham 66

Monkfish Skewers With Vegetables..... 67

Hamburger With French Fries 68

Egg To The Plate 69

Crashed Bones With Chips And Ham.... 70

Chapter 4: Poultry 71

Turkey And Cream Cheese Breast Pillows 71

Chicken Wings...................................... 72

Pickled Poultry 73

Cordon Bleu Chicken Breast................ 74

Fried Chicken.. 75

Rolls Stuffed With Broccoli And Carrots With Chicken 76

Chicken Flutes With Sour Sauce And Guacamole 78

Spicy Chicken Strips............................. 79

Chicken Breasts Covered With Parmesan Cheese.. 80

Chicken In Wheat Cake With Aioli Sauce 81

Soy Chicken And Sesame, Breaded And Fried 82

Chicken With Provencal Herbs And Potatoes 83

Chicken Tears 84

Breaded Chicken with Seed Chips.........85

Salted Biscuit Pie Turkey Chops 86

Lemon Chicken With Basil 87

Fried Chicken Tamari And Mustard 88

Breaded Chicken Fillets 89

Dry Rub Chicken Wings........................90

Mongolian Chicken Wings 91

Chicken Wings With Sriracha And Honey 92

Chicken Wings With Garlic Parmesan...93

Jerk Style Chicken Wings 94

Chicken Skewers With Garlic And Herb 95

Chicken Skewers With Yogurt...............96

Fried Lemon Chicken 97

Chicken's liver......................................98

Chicken Thighs......................................99

Chapter 5: Beef, Pork, Lamb Recipes100

Mediterranean Lamb Meatballs 100

Pork Rind 101

Pork Trinoza Wrapped In Ham............102

Homemade Flamingos........................103

North Carolina Style Pork Chops..........104

Beef With Sesame And Ginger............105

Katsu Pork..106

Pork On A Blanket................................107

Lamb Shawarma 108

Stuffed Cabbage And Pork Loin Rolls..109

Pork Head Chops With Vegetables 110

Provencal Ribs 111

Beef Scallops 112

Potatoes With Loin And Cheese 113

Potatoes With Loin And Cheese 114

Russian Steaks With Nuts And Cheese 115

Potatoes With Bacon, Onion And Cheese 116

Pork Liver 117

Marinated Loin Potatoes................... 118

Pork Fritters 119

Pork Tenderloin................................ 120

Cheesy Beef Pastelillo 121

Beef Patty... 122

Roasted Pork 123

Fried Pork Chops 124

Crispy Pork Chops 125

Pork Bondiola Chop.......................... 126

Pork Taquitos 127

Pork Knuckle 128

Chapter 6: Seafood and Fish recipes 130

Cajun Style Shrimp 130

Crab Cakes.. 131

Tuna Pie 133

Tuna Puff Pastry 134

Cajun Style Catfish........................... 135

Tuna Chipotle 136

Fish Tacos... 137

Teriyaki Glazed Salmon 138

Salmon With Butter And Lemon 139

Crispy Fish Nuggets 140

Bacon Wrapped Shrimp..................... 141

Coconut Shrimp 142

Easy Salmon...................................... 143

Hake With Roasted Peppers 144

Mushrooms Stuffed With Tuna 145

Hake Fillets With Salad 146

Hake Breaded With Red Peppers Cream 147

Breaded Hake With Green Chili Pepper And Mayonnaise................................ 148

Fried Anchovies 149

Roasted Peppers With Tuna Snacks.... 150

Tuna, Egg And Mozzarella Patties........ 151

Dye Fish With Tomato 152

Peppers Stuffed With Tuna................. 153

Hake Loins In Tempura 154

Cod Cakes 155

Mackerel In Fried Marinade 156

Fried Small Red Mullets 157

Fried Sardines 158

Crab Balls 159

Fried Squid 160

Fried Fish 161

Breaded Shrimp 162

Breaded Fish Fillet 163

Chapter 7: Vegan and Vegetarian Recipes 164

Homemade French Fries.................... 164

Sweet Potato Chips............................ 165

Cajun Style French Fries..................... 166

Fried Zucchini 167

Fried Avocado 168
Vegetables In air Fryer 169
Crispy Rye Bread Snacks With Guacamole And Anchovies................................. 170
Mushrooms Stuffed With Tomato 171
Spiced Potato Wedges 172
Egg Stuffed Zucchini Balls.................. 173
Vegetables With Provolone............... 174
Spicy Potatoes 175
Scrambled Eggs With Beans, Zucchini, Potatoes And Onions........................ 176
French Toast......................... 177
Sweet Potato Salt And Pepper 179
Potatoes With Provencal Herbs With Cheese................................. 180
Potato Wedges.................... 181
Onion Rings........................ 182
Onion Flower....................... 183
Hasselback Potatoes 184
Roasted Potatoes 185
Honey Roasted Carrots 186
Roasted Broccoli With Garlic............. 187
Roasted Cauliflower 188
Roasted Corn..................... 189
Roasted Pumpkin 190
Roasted Eggplant 191
Corn And Cheese Cakes..................... 192

Chapter 8: Desserts 193

Sweet Sponge Cake 193
Egg Flan............................... 194
Roasted Apples 195
Homemade Muffins............................ 196
Palm Trees Hojaldre 197
Chocolate And Nut Cake..................... 198
Light Cheese Cake With Strawberry Syrup 199
Banana And Nut Bread 200
Apple Mini Cakes 201
Rustic Pear Pie With Nuts 202
Lemon Biscuit 204
Cranberry And Lemon Muffins 205
Espresso Chocolate Muffins 206
Coconut Macaroni 207
Cranberry And Orange Muffins 208
Chocolate Chip Muffins 209
Cookies.. 210
Chocolate Churros 211
Roasted Banana................................ 212
Cupcake 213
Petit Gateau...................................... 214
Mini Cream Pump.............................. 215
Brownies... 216
Apple Pie... 217
Biscuits 219
Chocolate Cake 220
Gluten-Free Yogurt Cake 221

Conclusion 223

Introduction

The air fryer is one of the most impressive and useful inventions of the decade. With this machine, you can reduce the amount of grease you consume from traditional dishes and snacks such as chicken nuggets and French fries.

Many people still have their doubts regarding the importance of this machine, and what a healthy alternative it can be. Despite its popularity, in some regions it has not yet reached the peak of its use. It is very likely that in a short time new brands will emerge in other regions and the air fryer will grow in popularity across the nation.

The use of this tool consists of cooking something without boiling the product in oil or fat. At most, the maximum oil needed by the air fryer is a tablespoon, which is used to prevent the food from sticking and forming an overdone crust.

If you don't know how to use the air Fryer, don't despair. Once you have a complete idea about the essential functions of the air fryer in this first chapter, we will then discuss the different recipes you can cook up in an air fryer. For example:

- Chapter 2: Snacks and Appetizers
- Chapter 3: Breakfast Recipes
- Chapter 4: Poultry
- Chapter 5: Beef, Pork, Lamb Recipes
- Chapter 6: Seafood and Fish recipes
- Chapter 7: Vegan and Vegetarian Recipes
- Chapter 8: Desserts

In this eBook, you will learn all about the air fryer, along with over 200 recipes to try in your new cooking tool!

Enjoy the read!

Chapter 1: Air Fryer Basics

What is an air fryer?

An air fryer works with "fast air technology." This means that there is a high-speed circulation of hot air that cocoons the food you cook.. During this process, the air fryer prepares the food evenly, all the while giving it a "fried" taste and texture without ever actually having to fry anything in grease.

While many people and regions near and far are familiar with this tool, the electric fryer is even crossing the waters. They are even found commonly in Europe and Australia!

The air fryer is similar in concept to a convection oven or a turbo grill, although the fryer still differ slightly from both appliances.

Convection ovens and turbo broilers depend on different heating methods and are often larger and bulkier appliances to use when cooking your food.

How does an air fryer differ from a convection oven or a turbocharger?

While there's not much difference between the air fryer, turbocharger, and convection oven, there is enough difference to make it worth investigating to find the perfect fit for your personal needs.

Much like the air fryer, a convection oven circulates superheated air around the food, but there are very few portable/smaller-sized convection ovens, and usually, only the most expensive ones have a fan that circulates the air more evenly.

A turbo grill works using infrared/halogen light heat. As a radiant heat, it travels through the pot, and vice only rises as it does in a convection oven.

The air fryer uses an ingenious combination of both methods, differing from the convection oven because heat circulates everywhere (vice rising to the top) through the fan, and not through the turbo because there is typically no heating element in the top of a fryer from where the heat comes out. They use electrical energy to create their heat; a lot of power!

Characteristics of Air Fryers

Air Fryers in the market today vary in many of the features they offer. In general terms, halogen oven opinions fryers have the same right to fame: to provide consumers with the same flavor and texture of traditionally "fried" foods, but by using a fraction of the oil used by traditional fryers.

This characteristic not only makes them healthier for the heart, but also prevents many of the burns that can occur when it comes to getting the perfect fried foods.

Most air fryers offer a variety of cooking methods, and some have pre-programmed settings for cooking different types of food. You can cook so many things in an air fryer, including but not limited to meat, shrimp, chicken, and cakes.

What about pastries?

Yes! An advantage of the air fryer being similar in concept to a convection oven is to be able to 'bake' in an air fryer, but without needing the time, you would typically need to use a regular oven.

However, baking in an air fryer often requires a separate baking sheet, and currently, there are only two on the market that offer this accessory.

Some air fryers also promote their near-endless cooking functionalities by offering a reasonably cavernous kitchen space in comparison to their competing air fryers.

Why should you have one?

Why? The list is endless! There are some quite surprising reasons to have an air fryer in today's day and age. Although they try to isolate themselves as "oil-free" fryers, most air fryers have a lot of versatility in what they can be used for. They also offer quick and easy options for today's busy family looking to cook healthier meals.

air fryers also offer a reheating option that most broilers do not have, and air fryers are not as bulky as most other convection ovens.

The growing concerns about electromagnetic radiation in microwave ovens are sending more and more consumers looking for better ways to cook meals quickly, and an air fryer meets that demand.

The industry leader, Philips, manufactures different lines of air fryers. They are the best at the price level. While the cost of a good Philips air fryer might cause a consumer to hesitate, most of the customers swear they would not buy anything else. '

Another thing to take into consideration is capacity. If you are looking to feed a family of four or more people, you must invest in an air fryer that has the functionality to cook more food at once.

Most air fryers are ideal for one or two people, possibly three. However, many of them are not necessarily the perfect appliance for large family dishes.

Benefits of the air Fryer

What are the benefits of using an air fryer?

Calorie reduction: one of the main benefits attributed to these appliances is the considerable decrease in fat consumption. Unquestionably, when frying food in oil, you add many calories. This makes one of the most attractive benefits of an air fryer by reducing the calorie and fat consumption drastically, while still cooking the food to a delicious standard. air

Reduction in cooking time: With the programming of temperature and time, you can control the constant flow of hot air and accelerate the process of cooking food. This can save up to 40% of the time used in a regular frying process.

Reduction of energy expenditure: If you compare the energy consumption of the air fryer with that of a conventional electric oven, you will see that the consumption varies by a reasonably high percentage. You can save more than 50% of electrical energy when using the fryer! For example, the Philips air fryer consumes about 390Wh to fry half a kilo of potatoes. This is 45% less electricity than a conventional oven uses[1].

Saving money: when not using oil, it is a critical point to highlight that in your grocery purchases. You can achieve almost the same results without making that extra expense.

Ease of cleaning: With an air fryer, the cleaning process will be much easier or even null than the competing cookware depending on whether you want to spray oil or not before cooking. The container where the food is placed is removable, which makes it easy to wash and clean.

Based on all this, we can conclude that having an air fryer brings many advantages and benefits to the level of health, space inside the kitchen, and time. The air fryers are not limited only to frying food, as you can control the temperature. Time would also allow you to steam and cook, which is another significant benefit of having this appliance,

---

[1] https://www.hotairfrying.com/a-hot-air-fryer-is-not-necessarily-an-energy-saver/

especially if you do not have fried foods in your regular diet. These other cooking methods could also be achieved in less time than in other kitchen implements.

Tips for Using Your air Fryer

Regardless of the differences between models, you should always make sure to use only utensils that are manufactured and designed to fit in your appliance, as this will allow hot air to circulate efficiently. Below we have listed some tips to help the machine function to the best of its ability.

Tip #1: Adjust the cooking temperature

One of the first mistakes we make when we start using an air fryer is using the same temperature indicated for a recipe in which it is fried with oil, or in which the food is roasted. However, because the circulating air makes the cooking temperature more consistent, it is necessary to adjust the temperature of the air fryer by decreasing the indicated temperature by approximately 4°C, or 25°F.

You must not forget that the air fryer should be preheated, just like a conventional oven. Fortunately, this is a process that usually lasts less than five minutes. You must do this just before filling the basket, just as you do when baking.

Tip #2: Mix the ingredients with a moderate amount of oil

As a rule, you should mix your food with one or two tablespoons of oil, regardless of their nature, before placing them in the air fryer. The exception to this is for those foods that already contain fat themselves.

In the case of foods that have been passed through a mixture to breach or weather, it is advisable first to spray the basket with aerosol oil before layering the ingredients. Then, give them a last layer of oil on the higher part. By doing this, you will make them more golden and crispier.

Now, as an exception to the rule, frozen foods such as fish sticks, chicken nuggets, or pre-cooked potatoes do not need any oil added before putting them in the air fryer basket.

Tip #3: Avoid moisture in the ingredients

To use the air fryer, it is also advisable to perfectly drain those foods that, for example, have been previously marinated. By draining the foods appropriately, you will prevent excess smoke from forming. It's the same for when you're cooking those foods high in fat; you must make sure to remove the excess that remains at the bottom of the fryer periodically.

Tip #4: Don't overfill the rack

Cleaning Your air Fryer

It is crucial to maintain your air fryer, and you should clean it regularly to make sure it continues to work to the best of its availability. Below, we will show you what to do.

First, unplug your air fryer and let it cool before trying to clean it. Rub the outside with a built-in fagor fryer with a damp cloth.

The parts of the balay that are built into the air fryer are made of non-stick coating, so it is not necessary to clean them. However, if the food is stuck to the surface, it is recommended to soak it before washing.

How do I clean the metal utensils of a fryer?

Metal utensils should not be used when cleaning the air fryer, as it causes scratches and marks. Instead, you should use a non-abrasive sponge. Clean the pan, tray, and basket with warm water and dish soap. As all removable components are safe for essential dishwasher fryers, you can place them in the dishwasher to wash them. Use liquid soap degreaser for cleaning.

How do you clean the inside of the fryer?

It is essential to understand that the inner side of the airtight fryer may require a different type of cleaning. You can clean the inside with warm water and a sponge or cloth. Clean any food that is near the burner or that is above the food basket with a brush. You can use a filter to eliminate odors that are released. Remember to rinse the fryer regularly.

What should you do after cleaning?

Make sure that the tray and basket dry thoroughly before putting it back in the fryer. If the fryer has a persistent smell of food, clean it immediately. Even after cleaning, if there is still a smell, soak the pot and basket in a solution of liquid soap up to an hour before rinsing it again.

What should you do if the smell does not disappear?

Despite this, if the smell persists, you can cut a lemon in half and rub on the pan and basket or even squirt lemon juice on a paper towel and clean the fryer with it. After half an hour you can rewash. If white smoke comes out of the tray, this implies that there is too much grease on the bottom and that it is breaking due to the heat. Therefore, it needs to be cleaned well.

All these steps will be of great help for the air fryer to work correctly for a long time.

Chapter 2: Snacks and Appetizers

Bacon Chicken Roll

Preparation time: 5 minutes. Cooking time: 25 minutes. Serves: 4

Ingredients:

- 6 chicken breast ribs, cleaned
- 6 slices of bacon
- Garlic, salt, and black pepper to taste
- Wood sticks

Direction:

1. Preheat the air fryer. Set the time of 5 minutes and the temperature to 200^0C. At the end of that time, the air fryer will turn off.
2. Season the chicken with garlic, pepper, and salt to taste. Place each chicken roll on a slice of bacon and roll it. Prick with a stick to secure.
3. Place in the basket of the air fryer. Set the time of 20 minutes and press the power button. Shake the basket halfway through to get golden rolls evenly.
4. Once ready, transfer to a plate and serve

Nutritional Value (Amount per Servings):

- Calories: 217
- Proteins: 29.0g
- Carbohydrates: 5.8g
- Lipids: 8.8g
- Sugars: 0.6g
- Cholesterol: 80.4mg

Spicy Potato Chips

Preparation time: 5 minutes. Cooking time: 60 minutes. Serve: 5

Ingredients:

- 1 pound of red potatoes for cooking, in ½ inch (4 medium) pieces
- 2 tsp olive oil
- 1 tbsp cornmeal
- 1 tsp spicy condiments

Direction:

1. Put the potatoes in a large bowl, cover them with water, and let them soak for 30 minutes.
2. Drain them, dry them with paper towels, and return them to the bowl. Combine oil with cornmeal and seasonings in a small bowl. Pour the oil mixture over the potatoes and stir to cover them well.
3. Put the potatoes inside the basket. Cook at a temperature of 400°F for 26 to 30 minutes, stirring or stirring twice during cooking.

Nutrition Value (Nutrition per Serving):

- Calories: 112
- Fat: 7g
- Carbohydrates: 9g
- Protein: 1g
- Sugar: 0g
- Cholesterol: 0mg

Crispy Apple And Pear With Oatmeal

Preparation time: 5 minutes. Cooking time: 30 minutes. Serve: 4

Ingredients:

- ¼ cup plus 2 tbsp quick-cooking oatmeal
- 3 tbsp common flour
- 2 tbsp packed brown sugar
- ½ tsp ground condiments for pumpkin pies, divided
- 1½ tbsp butter in small pieces
- 1 medium apple (8 ounces) Golden Delicious, peeled, without center and chopped
- 1 medium pear (8 ounces), peeled and chopped
- 1 tsp lemon juice
- 4 ounces mascarpone cheese
- ½ tbsp of sugar
- ½ tsp vanilla essence

Direction:

1. Preheat the air fryer to a temperature of 350°F. Combine oatmeal, flour, brown sugar, and ¼ teaspoon of pumpkin pie seasonings in a medium bowl. Add the butter, and using your fingers or kneader, incorporating it until it becomes crumb; set it aside.

2. Mix the apple pieces and pears; Sprinkle with lemon juice and pumpkin pie seasonings. Pour this mixture into a 1-quart oven-safe container that fits comfortably inside the basket. Spray the reserved oatmeal mixture over the fruit pieces evenly. Cook for 30 minutes or until the fruit becomes soft. Remove the container from the fryer and let it cool slightly.

3. While the crunch is cooling, mix the mascarpone cheese, sugar, and vanilla in a small bowl. Put a portion of the mascarpone cheese mixture on the crunch.

Nutrition Value (Nutrition per Serving):

- Calories: 81
- Fat: 3g
- Carbohydrates: 12g
- Protein: 1g
- Sugar: 3g
- Cholesterol: 0mg

Buns With Carrots And Nuts

Preparation time: 5 minutes. Cooking time: 20 minutes. Serve: 4

Ingredients:

- ½ cup whole-grain flower
- ¼ cup of sugar
- ½ tsp baking soda
- ¼ tsp cinnamon
- ⅛ tsp nutmeg
- ½ cup grated carrots
- 2 tbsp chopped walnuts
- 2 tbsp grated coconut
- 2 tbsp golden raisins
- 1 egg
- 1 tbsp milk
- ½ tsp vanilla essence
- ¼ cup applesauce

Direction:

Preheat the fryer to a temperature of 350°F. Grease the bottom of 4 muffin molds or glass cups for custard, or magazine with muffin papers. Combine flour, sugar, baking soda, cinnamon, and nutmeg in a medium bowl. Add carrots, nuts, coconut, and raisins to the flour mixture.

Beat together the egg, milk, and vanilla in a small bowl. Add the applesauce. Put the flour mixture and stir until well incorporated.

Fill the prepared molds or cups with an equal amount of dough (⅓ cup) and then put them inside the basket. Cook for 15 minutes, then let them cool in the molds for 5 minutes before removing.

Nutrition Value (Nutrition per Serving):

- Calories: 195
- Fat: 11.04g
- Carbohydrates: 24.25g
- Protein: 2.22g
- Sugar: 15.15g
- Cholesterol: 67mg

Pine Skewers Aceto Reduction

Preparation time: 5 minutes. Cooking time: 15 minutes. Serve: 2

Ingredients:

- 1 small can of pineapple in its juice
- Necessary quantity Peeled prawns
- Skewers Sticks
- For the sauce:
- 150 ml of Balsamic Aceto
- 120g of sugar

Direction:

1. Open a small can of pineapple in its juice and drain well.
2. Cut the pineapple slices into four parts and set aside.
3. Peel the prawns and take out the tail.
4. Preheat the air fryer at 180^0C temperature for a few minutes and put the skewers in the basket. Program the timer about 10 minutes at 1800^0C.
5. To prepare the balsamic Aceto sauce: place the Aceto and sugar in a small pot. Reduce over low heat until it thickens but without letting caramel.
6. Let stand until it cools.

Nutritional Value (Amount per Serving):

- Calories: 226g
- Fat: 2g
- Carbohydrates: 36g
- Proteins: 16g
- Cholesterol: 156mg

Mini Burgers

Preparation time: 5 minutes. Cooking time: 25 minutes. Serve: 4

Ingredients:

- 500g Minced pork
- Salt
- Ground pepper
- Garlic Powder
- Fresh parsley
- Spices
- 1 egg
- 1 tbsp grated bread
- Mini Bread for Burgers

Direction:

1. Dress the meat of the hamburgers.
2. Add some salt to the ground beef, some ground pepper, garlic powder, a tablespoon of chopped fresh parsley, a teaspoon of spices.
3. Now, throw an egg and one or two teaspoons of breadcrumbs, so that the meat becomes more consistent. Stir all ingredients well until everything is integrated
4. Then, cover it with transparent and let it rest in the refrigerator for at least half an hour or more. It will be easier after handling the meat and giving it the shape of a hamburger.
5. Once the time has elapsed, take out the meat. Take it out of the paper that surrounds the container and begins to mold and make the mini burger.
6. To prepare them in the fryer:
7. First, heat the fryer. So, adjust the thermostat to 200^0C and the timer for about 5 minutes. When it is hot, the pilot or the green light will go out.
8. When half the time has passed, turn around so that they are done well by both parties.

Nutrition Value (Nutrition per Serving):

- Calories: 219
- Fat: 17g
- Carbohydrates: 0g
- Sugar: 0g
- Protein: 18g
- Cholesterol: 70 mg

Chicken Sandwich

Preparation time: 5 minutes. Cooking time: 15 minutes. Serve: 2

Ingredients:

- 2 cloves garlic
- Fresh parsley leaves
- 500g chopped breast
- 1 tsp Salt
- Pepper
- 1 egg L
- 50g milk
- 50g Cheese spread
- 14-16 slices sliced bread
- 7-8 slices semi-cured cheese

Direction:

1. Chop the garlic and parsley.
2. Add the breast in pieces, salt, and pepper
3. Add the rest of the ingredients and spread slices!
4. Spread the paste on all the slices, cover half with a slice of cheese, and cover with another slice, cut into triangles and there are two options, pass them by egg and breadcrumbs
5. Preheat the 220^0C air fryer, about 8 or 10 minutes, until the bread becomes colored.

Nutrition Value (Nutrition per Serving):

- Calories: 215
- Fat: 29.4g
- Carbohydrates: 38.7g
- Protein: 24.1g
- Assume: 0g
- Cholesterol: 60.1mg

Potato Balls Stuffed with Ham and Cheese From The air Fryer

Preparation time: 5 minutes. Cooking time: 25 minutes. Serve: 4

Ingredients:

- 4 potatoes
- 100g cooked ham
- 100g of grated or grated cheese
- Salt
- Ground pepper
- Flour
- Oil

Direction:

1. Peel the potatoes and cut into quarters.
2. Put in a pot with water and bring to the fire, let cook until tender.
3. Drain and squeeze with a fork until the potatoes are made dough and season.
4. Add the ham and cheese.
5. Let's link everything.
6. Make balls and pass through the flour.
7. Spray with oil and go to the basket of the air fryer.
8. Select 20 minutes, 200^0C for each batch of balls you put. Do not pile up because they would break down. From time to time remove from the basket so that they are made on all sides, you have to shake the basket so that the balls roll a little and serve.

Nutritional Value (Nutrition per Serving):

- Calories: 224
- Fat: 14g
- Carbohydrates: 19g
- Protein: 4g
- Sugar: 1g
- Cholesterol: 0mg

Spring Rolls

Preparation time: 5 minutes. Cooking time: 30 minutes. Serve: 6

Ingredients:

- 8 sheets of Philo pasta
- 2 onions
- 2 carrots
- 1 piece of Chinese cabbage
- 75g of bean sprouts
- Salt
- Ground pepper
- Extra virgin olive oil
- 1 dash of soy sauce

Direction:

1. Grate the carrots, cabbage, and onions.
2. Put in the Wok some extra virgin olive oil.
3. When it's hot, add the vegetables,
4. Season and sauté without losing the crunchy touch.
5. Incorporate the bean sprouts and the soy sauce.
6. Sauté and let temper so that the Philo pasta does not get very wet.
7. Extend the sheets, distribute the filling between the layers and roll up, in the form of a roll, that is, the filling in the center of the sheet. Give the first fold from the bottom up, then the sides mount them on top of each other, and now you end up spinning up its width.
8. Place in the basket of the air fryer, 2 in 2.
9. Paint with oil.
10. Select 20 minutes, 180^0C.
11. Make all the rolls.
12. When you have them all done, place all in the basket of the air fryer, one over the other carefully. Select 5 minutes, 180^0C, and give a heat stroke so that all are served hot.

Nutrition Value (Nutrition per Serving):

- Calories: 105
- Fat: 10g
- Carbohydrates: 3g
- Protein: 5g
- Sugar: 0g
- Cholesterol: 11mg

Sausages And Chorizos

Preparation time: 10 minutes. Cooking time: 20 minutes. Serve: 2-4

- 300g of sausage or frozen sausages
- One tablespoon olive oil

Direction:

1. Remove sausages directly from the freezer and place them in the fryer basket.
2. To defrost sausages and remove some of their fat, you must boil them for 5 to 10 minutes, and then prick food to remove all the remaining fat.
3. Then separate the sausages and chorizos on a tray or bowl.
4. Add a tablespoon of your favorite oil (preferably olive oil) in the bowl and mix the sausage well with the oil.
5. Then place the sausages and chorizos in the fryer basket.
6. Program your fryer at a temperature of 190°C and the timer in about 10 minutes.
7. Then turn the sausage as well as chorizos and perform the same process with the fryer.
8. And finally, after 10 minutes, serve and enjoy them.

Nutrition Value (Nutrition per Serving):

- Calories: 356
- Protein: 21.18g
- Fat: 29.30g
- Sugar: 1.90g
- Carbohydrates: 1.90g
- Cholesterol: 72.60mg

T-Bone Steak Santa Maria

Preparation time: 5 minutes. Cooking time: 15 minutes. Serve: 2

Ingredients:

- 2g of salt
- 2g black pepper
- 2g garlic powder
- 2g onion powder
- 2g dried oregano
- A pinch of dried rosemary
- A pinch of cayenne
- A pinch of dried sage
- 1 ribeye boneless
- 15 ml of olive oil

Direction:

1. Select Preheat in the air fryer and press Start/Pause
2. Mix the seasonings and sprinkle on the steak.
3. Spray olive oil on the steak.
4. Place the fillet in the preheated air fryer, select Steak, and press Start/Pause.
5. Remove the fillet from the air fryer when finished. Let stand for 10 minutes before cutting and serving.

Nutrition Value (Nutrition per Serving):

- Calories: 115
- Fat: 2.6g
- Carbohydrates: 1.8g
- Protein: 20.8
- Sugar: 0g

Steak with Chimichurri

Preparation time: 5 minutes. Cooking time: 20 minutes. Serve: 5

Ingredients:

- Fillet
- 12 ml of vegetable oil
- 16 oz Steak
- Salt and pepper to taste
- 60 ml of extra virgin olive oil
- 20g fresh basil
- 20g coriander
- 20g parsley
- 4 anchovy fillets
- 1 small shallot
- 2 cloves garlic, peeled
- 1 lemon, juiced
- A pinch of crushed red pepper

Direction:

1. Combine all the ingredients of the chimichurri sauce in a blender and mix until you reach the desired consistency.
2. Preheat the air fryer by pressing Start/Pause
3. Rub vegetable oil in the fryer on the steak and season with salt and pepper.
4. Place the fillet in the preheated air fryer.
5. Select Steak, set the time to 6 minutes (so that it is half cooked), and press Start/Pause.
6. Allow the steak to rest for 5 minutes when finished.
7. Finally, cover with chimichurri sauce and serve.

Nutrition Value (Nutrition per Serving):

- Calories: 333
- Fat: 20g
- Carbohydrate: 4g
- Protein: 34g
- Sugar: 1g
- Cholesterol: 104mg

Flank Steak with Balsamic Mustard

Preparation time: 10 minutes. Cooking time: 2h 15 minutes. Serve: 3

Ingredients:

- 60 ml of olive oil
- 60 ml balsamic vinegar
- 36g Dijon mustard
- 16 oz flank steak
- Salt and pepper to taste
- 4 basil leaves, sliced

Direction:

1. Mix olive oil, balsamic vinegar, and mustard. Mix them to create a marinade.
2. Put the steak directly in the marinade. Cover with plastic wrap and marinate in the fridge for 2 hours or at night.
3. Remove from the refrigerator and let it reach room temperature.
4. Preheat the air fryer by pressing Start/Pause.
5. Place the fillet in the preheated air fryer, select Fillet, and press Start/Pause.
6. Cut the steak at an angle through the muscle. Season with salt and pepper and decorate with the basil to serve.

Nutrition Value (Nutrition per Serving):

- Calories: 275
- Fat: 6.1g
- Carbohydrates: 18.8g
- Protein: 29.5g
- Sugar: 6g

Italian Meatballs

Preparation time: 5 minutes. Cooking time: 25 minutes. Serve: 4

Ingredients:

- 227g ground beef
- 28g of breadcrumbs
- 30 ml of milk
- 1 egg
- 3g garlic powder
- 2g onion powder
- 2g dried oregano
- 2g dried parsley
- Salt and pepper to taste
- 15g grated Parmesan cheese
- Spray oil

Direction:

1. Mix ground meat, breadcrumbs, eggs, spices, salt, pepper, and Parmesan.
2. Create small balls with the meat mixture. Place them in the refrigerator for 10 minutes.
3. Select Preheat in the air fryer and press Start/Pause.
4. Remove the meatballs from the refrigerator and place them in the baskets of the preheated air fryer. Spray the meatballs with oil spray and cook at 205°C for 8 minutes.
5. Serve with marinara sauce and grated Parmesan cheese.

Nutrition Value (Nutrition per Serving):

- Calories: 286
- Fat: 22.21g
- Carbohydrates: 18.1g
- Protein: 14.40g
- Sugar: 3.47g
- Cholesterol: 66mg

Japanese Meatballs

Preparation time: 10 minutes. Cooking time: 25 minutes. Serve: 3

Ingredients:

- 16 oz ground beef
- 15 ml sesame oil
- 18g miso paste
- 10 fresh mint leaves, finely chopped
- 4 scallions, finely chopped
- 5g of salt
- 1 g black pepper
- 45 ml of soy sauce
- 45 ml mirin
- 45 ml of water
- 3g brown sugar

Direction:

1. Mix the ground beef, sesame oil, miso paste, mint leaves, chives, salt, and pepper until everything is well bonded.
2. Add a small amount of sesame oil to your hands and create 51 mm meatballs with the mixture. You should have eight meatballs approximately.
3. Let the meatballs cool in the refrigerator for 10 minutes.
4. Create the sauce by mixing the soy sauce, the mirin, the water, and the brown sugar. Leave aside.
5. Preheat the air fryer by pressing Start/Pause.
6. Arrange the chilled meatballs in the preheated air fryer.
7. Select Steak set the time to 10 minutes and press Start/Pause.
8. Freely brush the meatballs with the glaze every 2 minutes.

Nutrition Value (Nutrition per Serving):

- Calories: 724
- Fat: 31g
- Carbohydrates: 80g
- Proteins: 31g
- Sugar: 0g

Mushroom Croquettes

Preparation time: 5 minutes. Cooking time: 25 minutes. Serve: 4

Ingredients:

- 200g mushrooms
- ¼ of an onion
- Salt
- Nutmeg
- 3 large tbsp of flour
- 4 tbsp oil or
- 40g butter
- 1 liter of skim milk
- Breadcrumbs
- 2 eggs
- Flour

Direction:

1. Chop the mushrooms and onion.
2. Brown the onion and mushrooms with a little oil in a pot, salt, and when golden brown, add two tablespoons of butter or a good stream of oil.
3. Add the tablespoons of flour and stir well until you get a very thick dough.
4. Gradually incorporate the milk (previously heated), until a dense mass is obtained.
5. Add salt and sprinkle with a pinch of nutmeg.
6. Let cool in the fridge for about two hours.
7. Make balls with the dough and pass through flour, egg, and breadcrumbs.
8. Preheat the air fryer a few minutes to 180^0C, and when ready, put the croquettes in the basket and set the timer for about 15 minutes at 180^0C.

Nutrition Value (Nutrition per Serving):

- Calories: 54
- Fat: 2g
- Carbohydrates: 7g
- Protein: 2
- Sugar: 1g
- Cholesterol: 12mg

Sausage Puff Pastry

Preparation time: 5 minutes. Cooking time: 20 minutes. Serve: 1-4

Ingredients:

- Amount needed of puff pastry
- Amount needed of sausages

Direction:

- Cut the puff pastry into thin slices about 5 cm wide.
- Divide the sausages into two pieces.
- Preheat the air fryer a few minutes at 180^0C.
- Meanwhile, roll each piece of sausage with a strip of puff pastry and paint on top with beaten egg.
- Place in the basket of the air fryer.
- Set the timer 10 minutes at 180^0C temperature.
- Take as an appetizer at any time of the year. Kids love it.

Nutrition Value (Nutrition per Serving):

- Calories: 135
- Protein: 4g
- Fat: 11g
- Sugar: 0g
- Carbohydrates: 5g
- Cholesterol: 23mg

Peppers Stuffed with Potato Omelet

Preparation time: 10 minutes. Cooking time: 25 minutes. Serve: 2

Ingredients:

- 2 large peppers (green, red)
- 2 medium potatoes
- 1 egg
- 1 tbsp olive oil
- Salt

Direction:

1. Preheat the air fryer about 4 minutes at 180^0C. While heating, peel and cut the potatoes as for tortillas. Go through plenty of water and dry thoroughly.
2. Spray the cut potatoes with a little olive oil and place in the fryer basket.
3. Insert the basket in the air fryer and set the timer to about 12 minutes to
4. 1800^0C temperature Stir the potatoes halfway through cooking.
5. While the potatoes are cooking, clean the peppers, cut the tops, and remove all the seeds. Spray the peppers with olive oil and lightly salt them.
6. When the potatoes are ready, salt them. Beat the egg and mix it with the potatoes.
7. Fill the peppers with this mixture and put them in the basket
8. Enter it again in the air fryer and program about 7 minutes at 200^0C.

Nutrition Value (Nutrition per Serving):

- Calories: 133
- Fat: 5g
- Carbohydrates: 17g
- Protein: 5g
- Sugar: 0g
- Cholesterol: 50 mg

Longaniza Skewers

Preparation time: 10 minutes. Cooking time: 25 minutes. Serve: 4

Ingredients:

- 4 fresh Tuscan sausages
- 2 peppers cut into squares
- 1 onion, cut into large cubes
- Coarse salt and pepper to taste
- 2 tbsp of brush oil
- Wooden skewers

Preparation:

1. Preheat the air fryer. Set the time of 5 minutes and the temperature to 200^0C.
2. At the end of the time, the air fryer will turn off.
3. Cut the sausages into thick slices with about 2 cm. Then season with salt and pepper.
4. Assemble the skewers alternating slices of sausage, peppers, and onions to finish all the ingredients. Let the skewers with about 12 cm to fit in the basket of the air fryer.
5. Cut the excess with kitchen scissors. Brush with olive oil and set aside.
6. Organize the skewers in the basket of the air fryer. Set the time of 20 minutes and press the power button.
7. After ready, transfer to a plate and serve.

Nutrition Value (Nutrition per Serving):

- Calories: 273
- Fat: 29.96g
- Carbohydrates: 1.12g
- Protein: 14.46g
- Sugar: 0g

Eggplant Milanese

Preparation time: 5 minutes. Cooking time: 40 minutes. Serve: 2

Ingredients:

- 1 medium eggplant
- 1 tbsp of vinegar
- 2 lightly beaten whole eggs
- 1 cup of tea flour
- 1 ½ cup breadcrumbs

Direction:

1. Wash the eggplants and cut into slices of 1 cm maximum thickness, place the slices in a bowl with water and vinegar and let them soak for at least 15 minutes.
2. Preheat the air fryer. Set the time of 5 minutes and the temperature to 200 degrees.
3. Remove water from eggplant slices and place on a roasting pan, sprinkle salt to taste. Pass each slice through the flour, then through the beaten egg and finally in breadcrumbs and squeezing the fingers and hands, so they remain very compact.
4. Place the eggplant slices in the basket of the air fryer and set the timer for 18 minutes and press the power button. Open the time in half to see if the weather needs an adjustment because the eggplants should be crispy on the outside and soft on the inside.

Nutrition Value (Nutrition per Serving):

- Calories: 103
- Fat: 5.61g
- Carbohydrates: 11.61g
- Protein: 2.4g
- Sugar: 2.45
- Cholesterol: 14mg

Potato Croquettes

Preparation time: 5 minutes. Cooking time: 25 minutes. Serve: 4

Ingredients:

- 300g of starchy potatoes, peeled and diced
- 1 egg yolk
- 50g grated Parmesan cheese
- 2 tbsp flour
- 2 tbsp chopped chives
- Freshly ground pepper
- Nutmeg
- 2 tbsp vegetable oil
- 50g of breadcrumbs

Direction:

1. Boil the potato dice in salted water for 15 minutes until they are tender. Drain them and mash them well with a potato masher or a Pasteur. Let them cool.
2. Add the egg yolk, cheese, flour, and chives to the mashed potatoes and mix well — season to taste with salt, pepper, and nutmeg.
3. Preheat the air fryer to 200°C. Mix the oil and breadcrumbs and continue stirring until the mixture is again loose and uniform.
4. Form 12 croquettes with the mashed potatoes and pass them on the breadcrumbs until they are well breaded.
5. Place six croquettes in the fryer basket and place it in the air fryer. Set the timer to 4 minutes and fry the potato croquettes until golden brown.

Nutrition Value (Nutrition per Serving):

- Calories: 301
- Fat: 18.5g
- Carbohydrates: 30.5g
- Protein: 3g
- Sugar: 0.54g

Stuffed Potatoes

Preparation time: 10 minutes. Cooking time: 25 minutes. Serve: 2

Ingredients:

- 2 large potatoes 25 x 25 cm
- ½ liter of water
- 2 tbsp butter tea soup
- 1 cup cream cheese
- ½ cup smoked turkey breast tea
- ½ cup mozzarella cheese

Direction:

- Wash the potatoes, then make several deep holes in it with a fork, wrap in potato paper. Cook the potatoes in a pressure cooker with ½ liter of water for 10 minutes.
- Preheat the air fryer. Set the time of 5 minutes and the temperature to 200^0C.
- Remove the potatoes from the pressure cooker. Open the foil only at the top, where the cut is made.
- With a knife, make a cut at the top to the middle of the potato and squeeze it lengthwise to leave more open. Sprinkle some salt. Place a spoonful of butter. Distribute half of the cream cheese and smoked turkey. Top with grated mozzarella cheese. Place in the basket of the air fryer and set the timer for 8 minutes and press the power button. Remove the potatoes from the air fryer using a thermal sleeve. Serve at the same time.

Nutrition Value (Nutrition per Serving):

- Calories: 77
- Fat: 0.2g
- Carbohydrates: 16g
- Protein: 1.7g
- Sugar: 1g

Cottage Cheese Spinach Cakes

Preparation time: 5 minutes. Cooking time: 15 minutes. Serve: 2

Ingredients:

- ½ cup of tea with milk
- ½ cup of tea oil
- ¾ cup flour
- 1 tsp of baking powder
- Salt to taste
- 1 cup cooked and chopped spinach
- ½ cup cottage cheese
- Grated cheese to sprinkle

Direction:

1. Preheat the air fryer. Set the time of 5 minutes and the temperature to 200^0C.
2. Beat all the ingredients except the cheese in your blender until smooth. Fill 1/3 each of silicone or aluminum shape with the dough. Fill with one spoon of curd tea. Cover with an additional portion of the dough.
3. Sprinkle with grated cheese.
4. Place six individual shapes in the basket of the air fryer. Set the time of 10 minutes and press the power button. At half time, check to see if they are already with golden surface and well-cooked inside. If necessary, adjust the preparation time.

Nutrition Value (Nutrition per Serving):

- Calories: 478
- Fat: 29g
- Carbohydrates: 39g
- Protein: 15g
- Sugar: 0g
- Cholesterol: 55mg

Crispy Tofu

Preparation time: 5 minutes. Cooking time: 20 minutes. Serve: 3

Ingredients:

- 225g firm tofu cut into 25 mm cubes
- 30 ml of soy sauce
- 10 ml of rice vinegar
- 10 ml sesame oil
- 40g cornstarch

Direction:

1. Mix the tofu, soy sauce, rice vinegar, and sesame oil in a shallow bowl. Let it macerate for 10 minutes.
2. Select Preheat, in the air fryer, set the temperature to 190°C and press Start/Pause.
3. Drain the tofu from the marinade and then place the tofu in corn starch until it is well covered.
4. Place the tofu in the preheated air fryer. Select Shrimp, set the time to 18 minutes press Start/Pause. Shake the baskets in the middle of cooking.

Nutrition Value (Nutrition per Serving):

- Calories: 78
- Fat: 4.96g
- Carbohydrates: 2.08g
- Protein: 7.82
- Sugar: 0.33g
- Cholesterol: 0

Ripe Bananas Croquettes

Preparation time: 10 minutes. Cooking time: 20 minutes. Serve: 6

Ingredients:

- 2 or 3 ripe bananas
- ½ tsp sugar per banana
- ½ tsp ground cinnamon
- Olive or coconut oil

- **Optional**:
- 1 tbsp grated cheese per banana
- 1 tbsp custard per banana

Direction:

1. Peel the bananas. Cut them in two and split them in the center.
2. Add sugar, cinnamon, and oil to each.
3. Place them in the air fryer tray.
4. Cook for 15-20 minutes at 180^0F until golden brown.
5. Optional: add mozzarella cheese in the last 5 minutes to melt and brown. They can also be served with custard.

Nutrition Value (Nutrition per Serving):

- Calories: 122
- Fat: 0.37g
- Carbohydrates: 31.89g
- Protein: 1.3g
- Sugar: 15g
- Cholesterol: 0mg

Avocado Stuffed with Prawns

Preparation time: 5 minutes. Cooking time: 25 minutes. Serve: 4

Ingredients:

- 2 ripe avocados
- 6 tbsp lemon juice
- 2 cups clean and pre-cooked prawns
- 2 tbsp red onion, finely chopped
- 1 clove garlic finely chopped
- ¼ cup red paprika
- Salt and pepper to taste
- ½ cup parmesan cheese

Direction:

1. Split the avocados into two parts, remove the seeds and with a spoon carefully separate the pulp from the shell without removing it from it.
2. To each half pour 1 tbsp of lemon juice and reserve.
3. Mix the prawns with the onion, garlic, paprika, and add the remaining lemon; season with salt and pepper.
4. Place the shrimp mixture in the center of each avocado half and add the Parmesan cheese on top.
5. Place them in the cooking basket of the air fryer and set for 5 minutes at 200°C. Accompany them with fresh vegetables.

Nutrition Value (Nutrition per Serving):

- Calories: 97.5
- Fats: 2.2
- Carbohydrates: 10.3
- Proteins: 6.2

Broccoli and Cheese Croquettes

Preparation time: 15 minutes. Cooking time: 20 minutes. Serve: 6

Ingredients:

- 250g Broccoli
- ½ Onion
- 5-6 tbsp grated Parmesan cheese.
- 1 egg
- Breadcrumbs.
- 400 ml of milk
- 4 tbsp flour
- 3 tbsp olive oil
- Salt and pepper

Direction:

1. Cut the broccoli florets, discarding on the trunk. Put plenty of water in a saucepan and put it on the fire until it starts to boil. Incorporate the broccoli and cook it. Drain it and cut it into small pieces. Chop the onion into very fine pieces.

2. Add three tablespoons of olive oil in a pan and heat over medium heat. Add the chopped onion and wait until it becomes transparent. Lower the heat, add the flour, and stir until lightly browned.

3. Before the milk comes into play, heat it so that it is warm. Then add a glass of milk in the pan (in principle) next to the broccoli. Stir gently and without pause until it thickens.

4. Add the rest of the milk little by little and continue stirring as before. In turn, add Parmesan cheese, ground pepper, and salt to taste. When the dough has a thick consistency, turn off the heat, cover it with a lid so that it does not dry out and let it cool completely.

5. Take two deep plates. In one, beat an egg, and in the other, fill it with breadcrumbs. Take portions of dough and give it a croquette shape with your hands. To breach them first, pass them through the beaten egg (using a spoon) and then pass them through the breadcrumbs.

6. Put the croquettes in the basket and pulverized olive oil on top. Put the drawer and select 160^0C, 10 minutes. Take out the drawer, shake to move the croquettes, and select 180^0C and ten more minutes.

Nutrition Value (Nutrition per Serving):

- Calories: 359
- Fat: 32g
- Net carbohydrates: 6 g
- Fiber: 3g
- Protein: 11g

Sweet Potato Pie

Preparation time: 10 minutes. Cooking time: 1h 5 minutes. Serve: 2

Ingredients:

- 1 large sweet potato or 2 medium sweet potatoes
- 1 ½ cup ground or crushed whole oats (oatmeal)
- 1 egg white
- Salt, pepper, oregano to taste
- 1 tbsp olive oil or melted butter
- ¾ cup ricotta cheese
- 1 cup spinach
- ½ cup mushrooms
- ¼ cup chopped onion

Direction:

1. Cut the sweet potato in half, and on a tray with a little spray oil, put both halves upside down and bake for 40 minutes. (You can also boil the sweet potato)
2. With a tender, remove the pulp from the sweet potato and mash it (mash it, do not add anything else)
3. In a bowl, mix the sweet potato, oatmeal, salt, pepper, oregano, oil, and egg white.
4. Mix with your hands or a fork until getting dough. If you see it very dry, you can add a splash of water so that it takes better consistency.
5. In a pan, sauté the onion, mushrooms, spinach, and ricotta cheese. Add salt at your wish.
6. To form balls with the dough, and to strip them to be able to fill them.
7. Fill each circle with a tablespoon of the cheese, spinach, and mushroom mixture. Close in the form of pie.
8. Put in the air fryer 10 minutes at 200^0F to 15 minutes or until golden brown.

Nutrition Value (Nutrition per Serving):

- Calories: 92
- Fat: 2.3g
- Carbohydrates: 13g
- Protein: 4.5g
- Sugar: 6g
- Cholesterol: 6mg

Chapter 3: Breakfast Recipes

Cocotte Eggs

Preparation time: 5 minutes. Cooking time: 15 minutes. Serve: 1

Ingredients:

- 1 tbsp olive oil soup
- 2 tbsp crumbly ricotta
- 1 tbsp parmesan cheese soup
- 1 slice of gorgonzola cheese
- 1 slice of Brie cheese
- 1 tbsp cream soup
- 1 egg
- Nutmeg and salt to taste
- Butternut to taste

Direction:

1. Spread with olive oil in the bottom of a small glass refractory. Place the cheese in the bottom and season with nutmeg and salt. Add the cream.
2. Break the egg into a cup and gently add it to the refractory mixture.
3. Preheat the air fryer for the time of 5 minutes and the temperature at 200C. Put the refractory in the basket of the air fryer, set the time to 10 minutes, and press the power button. Remove and serve still hot.

Nutritional Value (Nutrition per Serving):

- Calories: 163
- Fat: 11g
- Carbohydrates: 3g
- Proteins: 13g
- Cholesterol: 336mg
- Sodium: 146mg

Tortilla

Preparation time: 10 minutes. Cooking time: 20 minutes. Serve: 2

Ingredients:

- 2 eggs
- 2 slices of ham, chopped
- 2 slices of chopped mozzarella
- 1 tbsp chopped onion soup
- ½ cup chopped parsley and chives tea
- Salt, black pepper and oregano to taste
- Olive oil spread

Direction:

1. Preheat the air fryer for the time of 5 minutes and the temperature at 200C.
2. Spread a refractory that fits in the basket of the air fryer and has a high shelf and reserve.
3. In a bowl, beat the eggs lightly with a fork. Add the fillings and spices. Place the refractory container in the basket of the air fryer and pour the beaten eggs being careful not to fall.
4. Set the time from 10 to 15 minutes and press the power button. The tortilla is ready when it is golden brown.

Nutrition Value (Nutrition per Serving):

- Calories: 41
- Fat: 1.01g
- Carbohydrates: 6.68g
- Protein: 1.08g
- Sugar: 0.25g
- Cholesterol: 0mg

Santa Fe Style Pizza

Preparation time: 10 minutes. Cooking time: 10 minutes. Serve: 2

Ingredients:

- 1 tsp vegetable oil
- ½ tsp ground cumin
- 2 tortillas 7 to 8 inches in diameter
- ¼ cup black bean sauce prepared
- 4 ounces cooked chicken, in strips or grated
- 1 tbsp taco seasonings
- 2 tbsp prepared chipotle sauce, or preferred sauce
- ¼ cup plus 2 tbsp corn kernels, fresh or frozen (thawed)
- 1 tbsp sliced scallions
- 1 tsp chopped cilantro
- ⅔ cup grated pepper jack cheese

Direction:

1. Put the oil with the cumin in a small bowl; spread the mixture on both tortillas. Then spread the black bean sauce evenly over both tortillas. Put the chicken pieces and taco seasonings in medium bowl; Stir until chicken is covered. Add the sauce and mix it with the covered chicken.

2. Remove half of the chicken and place it over the bean sauce in one of the tortillas. Put half the corn, chives, and cilantro over the tortilla and then cover with half the cheese. Put the pizza inside the basket and cook it at a temperature of 400°F for 10 minutes. Prepare the other tortilla and cook it after removing the first one.

Nutrition Value (Nutrition per Serving):

- Calories: 285
- Fat: 10.4g
- Carbohydrates: 35.7g
- Protein: 12.2g
- Sugar: 3.8g
- Cholesterol: 18.2mg

Grilled Sandwich With Three Types Of Cheese

Preparation time: 10 minutes. Cooking time: 8 minutes. Serve: 2

Ingredients:

- 2 tbsp mayonnaise
- ⅛ tsp dried basil
- ⅛ tsp dried oregano
- 4 slices of whole wheat bread
- 2 slices of ½ to 1-ounce cheddar cheese
- 2 slices of Monterey Jack cheese
- ½ to 1 ounce
- 2 thin slices of tomato
- 2 slices of ½ to 1 oz provolone cheese Soft butter

Direction:

1. Mix mayonnaise with basil and oregano in a small bowl and then spread the mixture on each side of the slice. Cover each slice with a slice of each cheese and tomato, and then the other slice of bread.
2. Lightly brush each side of the sandwich and put the sandwiches in the basket. Cook at a temperature of 400°F for 8 minutes, turning halfway through cooking.

Nutrition Value (Nutrition per Serving):

- Calories: 1431
- Fat: 20.67g
- Carbohydrates: 27.86g
- Protein: 13.88g
- Sugar: 4.35g
- Cholesterol: 33mg

Sweet Nuts Butter

Preparation time: 5 minutes. Cooking time: 25 minutes. Serve: 5

Ingredients:

- 1½ pounds sweet potatoes, peeled and cut into ½ inch pieces (2 medium)
- ½ tbsp olive oil
- 1 tbsp melted butter
- 1 tbsp finely chopped walnuts
- ½ tsp grated one orange
- ⅛ tsp nutmeg
- ⅛ tsp ground cinnamon

Direction:

1. Put sweet potatoes in a small bowl and sprinkle with oil. Stir until covered and then pour into the basket, ensuring that they are in a single layer. Cook at a temperature of 350°F for 20 to 25 minutes, stirring or turning halfway through cooking. Remove them to the serving plate. Combine the butter, nuts, orange zest, nutmeg, and cinnamon in a small bowl and pour the mixture over the sweet potatoes.

Nutrition Value (Nutrition per Serving):

- Calories: 1,682.56
- Fat: 10.25g
- Carbohydrates: 7.89g
- Protein: 5.01g
- Sugar: 6.31g
- Cholesterol: 0.43mg

Zucchini And Walnut Cake With Maple Flavor Icing

Preparation time: 5 minutes. Cooking time: 35 minutes. Serve: 5

Ingredients:

- 1 9-ounce package of yellow cake mix
- 1 egg
- ⅓ cup of water
- ½ cup grated zucchini
- ¼ cup chopped walnuts
- ¾ tsp of cinnamon
- ¼ tsp nutmeg
- ¼ tsp ground ginger
- Maple Flavor Glaze

Direction:

2. Preheat the fryer to a temperature of 350°F. Prepare an 8 x 3⅞ inch loaf pan. Prepare the cake dough according to package directions, using ⅓ cup of water instead of ½ cup. Add zucchini, nuts, cinnamon, nutmeg, and ginger.

3. Pour the dough into the prepared mold and put it inside the basket. Bake until a toothpick inserted in the middle of the cake is clean when removed for 32 to 34 minutes.

4. Remove the cake from the fryer and let it cool on a grill for 10 minutes. Then, remove the cake and place it on a serving plate. Stop cooling just warm. Spray it with maple flavor glaze.

Nutrition Value (Nutrition per Serving):

- Calories: 196
- Carbohydrates: 27g
- Fat: 11g
- Protein: 1g
- Sugar: 7g
- Cholesterol: 0mg

Misto Quente

Preparation time: 5 minutes. Cooking time: 10 minutes. Serve: 4

Ingredients:

- 4 slices of bread without shell
- 4 slices of turkey breast
- 4 slices of cheese
- 2 tbsp cream cheese
- 2 spoons of butter

Direction:

1. Preheat the air fryer. Set the timer of 5 minutes and the temperature to 200C.
2. Pass the butter on one side of the slice of bread, and on the other side of the slice, the cream cheese.
3. Mount the sandwiches placing two slices of turkey breast and two slices cheese between the breads, with the cream cheese inside and the side with butter.
4. Place the sandwiches in the basket of the air fryer. Set the timer of the air fryer for 5 minutes and press the power button.

Nutrition Value (Nutrition per Serving):

- Calories: 340
- Fat: 15g
- Carbohydrates: 32g
- Protein: 15g
- Sugar: 0g
- Cholesterol: 0mg

Garlic Bread

Preparation time: 10 minutes. Cooking time: 15 minutes. Serve: 4-5

Ingredients:

- 2 stale French rolls
- 4 tbsp crushed or crumpled garlic
- 1 cup of mayonnaise
- Powdered grated Parmesan
- 1 tbsp olive oil

Direction:

1. Preheat the air fryer. Set the time of 5 minutes and the temperature to 2000C.
2. Mix mayonnaise with garlic and set aside.
3. Cut the baguettes into slices, but without separating them completely.
4. Fill the cavities of equals. Brush with olive oil and sprinkle with grated cheese.
5. Place in the basket of the air fryer. Set the timer to 10 minutes, adjust the temperature to 1800C and press the power button.

Nutrition Value (Nutrition per Serving):

- Calories: 151
- Fat: 7.1g
- Carbohydrates: 17.9g
- Protein: 3.6g
- Sugar: 1.6g
- Cholesterol: 0mg

Bruschetta

Preparation time: 5 minutes. Cooking time: 10 minutes. Serve: 2

Ingredients:

- 4 slices of Italian bread
- 1 cup chopped tomato tea
- 1 cup grated mozzarella tea
- Olive oil
- Oregano, salt, and pepper
- 4 fresh basil leaves

Direction:

1. Preheat the air fryer. Set the timer of 5 minutes and the temperature to 2000C.
2. Sprinkle the slices of Italian bread with olive oil. Divide the chopped tomatoes and mozzarella between the slices. Season with salt, pepper, and oregano.
3. Put oil in the filling. Place a basil leaf on top of each slice.
4. Put the bruschetta in the basket of the air fryer being careful not to spill the filling. Set the timer of 5 minutes, set the temperature to 180C, and press the power button.
5. Transfer the bruschetta to a plate and serve.

Nutrition Value (Nutrition per Serving):

- Calories: 434
- Fat: 14g
- Carbohydrates: 63g
- Protein: 11g
- Sugar: 8g
- Cholesterol: 0mg

Cream Buns with Strawberries

Preparation time: 10 minutes. Cooking time: 12 minutes. Serving: 6

Ingredients:

- 240g all-purpose flour
- 50g granulated sugar
- 8g baking powder
- 1g of salt
- 85g chopped cold butter
- 84g chopped fresh strawberries
- 120 ml whipping cream
- 2 large eggs
- 10 ml vanilla extract
- 5 ml of water

Direction:

1. Sift flour, sugar, baking powder and salt in a large bowl. Put the butter with the flour using a blender or your hands until the mixture resembles thick crumbs.
2. Mix the strawberries in the flour mixture. Set aside for the mixture to stand. Beat the whipping cream, 1 egg and the vanilla extract in a separate bowl.
3. Put the cream mixture in the flour mixture until they are homogeneous, then spread the mixture to a thickness of 38 mm.
4. Use a round cookie cutter to cut the buns. Spread the buns with a combination of egg and water. Set aside
5. Preheat the air fryer, set it to 180°C.
6. Place baking paper in the preheated inner basket.
7. Place the buns on top of the baking paper and cook for 12 minutes at 180°C, until golden brown.

Nutrition Value (Nutrition per Serving):

- Calories: 150
- Fat: 6g
- Carbohydrates: 24g
- Protein: 1g
- Sugar: 13g
- Cholesterol: 0mg

Blueberry Buns

Preparation time: 10 minutes. Cooking time: 12 minutes. Serving: 6

Ingredients:

- 240g all-purpose flour
- 50g granulated sugar
- 8g baking powder
- 2g of salt
- 85g chopped cold butter
- 85g of fresh blueberries
- 3g grated fresh ginger
- 113 ml whipping cream
- 2 large eggs
- 4 ml vanilla extract
- 5 ml of water

Direction:

1. Put sugar, flour, baking powder and salt in a large bowl.
2. Put the butter with the flour using a blender or your hands until the mixture resembles thick crumbs.
3. Mix the blueberries and ginger in the flour mixture and set aside
4. Mix the whipping cream, 1 egg and the vanilla extract in a different container.
5. Put the cream mixture with the flour mixture until combined.
6. Shape the dough until it reaches a thickness of approximately 38 mm and cut it into eighths.
7. Spread the buns with a combination of egg and water. Set aside Preheat the air fryer, set it to 180°C.
8. Place baking paper in the preheated inner basket and place the buns on top of the paper. Cook for 12 minutes at 180°C, until golden brown

Nutrition Value (Nutrition per Serving):

- Calories: 105
- Fat: 1.64g
- Carbohydrates: 20.09g
- Protein: 2.43g
- Sugar: 2.1g
- Cholesterol: 0mg

Cooked Egg in Casserole

Preparation time: 3 minutes. Cooking time: 14 minutes. Serving: 3

Ingredients:

- Nonstick Spray Oil
- 3 eggs
- 6 slices smoked bacon, diced
- 60g washed baby spinach
- 120 ml whipping cream
- 15g grated Parmesan cheese
- Salt and pepper to taste

Direction:

1. Preheat the air fryer, set it to 175°C.
2. Spray three 76 mm molds with nonstick spray oil.
3. Add 1 egg to each greased mold.
4. Cook the bacon in a pan until golden brown, about 5 minutes.
5. Add spinach and cook until wilted, 2 minutes.
6. Mix the whipping cream and Parmesan cheese. Cook for 2-3 minutes.
7. Pour the cream mixture over the eggs.
8. Place the molds in the preheated air fryer and cook for 4 minutes at 175°C until the egg white is fully prepared and season to taste with salt and pepper.

Nutrition Value (Nutrition per Serving):

- Calories: 635
- Fat: 2g
- Carbohydrates: 61g
- Protein: 19.5g
- Sugar: 0g
- Cholesterol: 40mg

French Toast in Sticks

Preparation time: 5 minutes. Cooking time: 10 minutes. Portion: 4

Ingredients:

- 4 slices of white bread, 38 mm thick, preferably hard
- 2 eggs
- 60 ml of milk
- 15 ml maple sauce
- 2 ml vanilla extract
- Nonstick Spray Oil
- 38g of sugar
- 3 ground cinnamon
- Maple syrup, to serve
- Sugar to sprinkle

Direction:

1. Cut each slice of bread into thirds making 12 pieces. Place sideways
2. Beat the eggs, milk, maple syrup and vanilla.
3. Preheat the air fryer, set it to 175°C.
4. Dip the sliced bread in the egg mixture and place it in the preheated air fryer. Sprinkle French toast generously with oil spray.
5. Cook French toast for 10 minutes at 175°C. Turn the toast halfway through cooking.
6. Mix the sugar and cinnamon in a bowl.
7. Cover the French toast with the sugar and cinnamon mixture when you have finished cooking.
8. Serve with Maple syrup and sprinkle with powdered sugar

Nutrition Value (Nutrition per serving):

- Calories: 159
- Fat: 6.13g
- Carbohydrates: 20.02g
- Protein: 5.58g
- Sugar: 4.87g
- Cholesterol: 90 mg

Muffins Sandwich

Preparation time: 2 minutes. Cooking time: 10 minutes. Serving: 1

Ingredients:

- Nonstick Spray Oil
- 1 slice of white cheddar cheese
- 1 slice of Canadian bacon
- 1 English muffin, divided
- 15 ml hot water
- 1 large egg
- Salt and pepper to taste

Direction:

1. Spray the inside of an 85g mold with oil spray and place it in the air fryer.
2. Preheat the air fryer, set it to 160°C.
3. Add the Canadian cheese and bacon in the preheated air fryer.
4. Pour the hot water and the egg into the hot pan and season with salt and pepper.
5. Select Bread, set to 10 minutes.
6. Take out the English muffins after 7 minutes, leaving the egg for the full time.
7. Build your sandwich by placing the cooked egg on top of the English muffing and serve

Nutrition Value (Nutrition per Serving):

- Calories: 400
- Fat: 26g
- Carbohydrates: 26g
- Protein: 15g
- Sugar: 3g
- Cholesterol: 155mg

Streusel Coffee Muffins

Preparation time: 10 minutes. Cooking time: 12 minutes. Serving: 6

Ingredients:

Crispy Deck

- 13g white sugar
- 16g light brown sugar
- 1g of cinnamon
- 2g of salt
- 14g unsalted butter, melted
- 24g all-purpose flour

Muffin

- 90g all-purpose flour
- 53g light brown sugar
- 4g baking powder
- 1g of baking soda
- 2g cinnamon
- 1g of salt
- 112 g sour cream
- 42g unsalted butter, melted
- 1 egg
- 4 ml vanilla extract
- Nonstick Spray Oil

Direction:

1. Mix all the ingredients of the crispy cover until they form thick crumbs. Set aside. Put the flour, brown sugar, baking powder, baking soda, cinnamon, and salt in a large bowl. Mix sour cream, butter, egg, and vanilla in a separate bowl until combined. Mix the wet ingredients with the dry ingredients until well combined.

2. Preheat the air fryer, set it to 175°C. Grease the muffin pans with oil spray and pour the mixture until the cups are 3/4.

3. Sprinkle the top of the muffins with the crispy topping. Place the muffin molds in the preheated air fryer. You may have to work in batches. Cook the muffins at 175°C for 12 minutes.

Nutrition Value (Nutrition per serving):

- Calories: 100
- Fat: 3g
- Carbohydrates: 21g
- Protein: 2g
- Sugar: 7g
- Cholesterol: 10mg

Bacon BBQ

Preparation time: 2 minutes. Cooking time: 8 minutes. Portion: 2

Ingredients:

- 13g dark brown sugar
- 5g chili powder
- 1g ground cumin
- 1g cayenne pepper
- 4 slices of bacon, cut in half

Direction:

1. Mix seasonings until well combined.
2. Dip the bacon in the dressing until it is completely covered. Leave aside.
3. Preheat the air fryer, set it to 160°C.
4. Place the bacon in the preheated air fryer
5. Select Bacon and press Start/Pause.

Nutrition Value (Nutrition per Serving):

- Calories: 1124
- Fat: 72g
- Carbohydrates: 59g
- Protein: 49g
- Sugar: 11g
- Cholesterol: 77mg

Breakfast Pizza

Preparation time: 5 minutes. Cooking time: 8 minutes. Serving: 1-2

Ingredients:

- 10 ml of olive oil
- 1 prefabricated pizza dough (178 mm)
- 28g low moisture mozzarella cheese
- 2 slices smoked ham
- 1 egg
- 2g chopped cilantro

Direction:

1. Pass olive oil over the prefabricated pizza dough.
2. Add mozzarella cheese and smoked ham in the dough.
3. Preheat the air fryer, set it to 175°C.
4. Place the pizza in the preheated air fryer and cook for 8 minutes at 175°C.
5. Remove the baskets after 5 minutes and open the egg on the pizza.
6. Replace the baskets in the air fryer and finish cooking. Garnish with chopped coriander and serve.

Nutrition Value (Nutrition per Serving):

- Calories: 224
- Fat: 7.5g
- Carbohydrates: 25.2g
- Protein: 14g
- Sugar: 0g
- Cholesterol: 13mg

Stuffed French Toast

Preparation time: 4 minutes. Cooking time: 10 minutes. Serving: 1

Ingredients:

- 1 slice of brioche bread,
- 64 mm thick, preferably rancid
- 113g cream cheese
- 2 eggs
- 15 ml of milk
- 30 ml whipping cream
- 38g of sugar
- 3g cinnamon
- 2 ml vanilla extract
- Nonstick Spray Oil
- Pistachios chopped to cover
- Maple syrup, to serve

Direction:

1. Preheat the air fryer, set it to 175°C.
2. Cut a slit in the middle of the muffin.
3. Fill the inside of the slit with cream cheese. Leave aside.
4. Mix the eggs, milk, whipping cream, sugar, cinnamon, and vanilla extract.
5. Moisten the stuffed French toast in the egg mixture for 10 seconds on each side.
6. Sprinkle each side of French toast with oil spray.
7. Place the French toast in the preheated air fryer and cook for 10 minutes at 175°C
8. Stir the French toast carefully with a spatula when you finish cooking.
9. Serve topped with chopped pistachios and acrid syrup.

Nutrition Value (Nutrition per Serving):

- Calories: 159
- Fat: 6.13g
- Carbohydrates: 20.02g
- Protein: 5.58g
- Sugar: 50g
- Cholesterol: 90 mg

Pepperoni Pizza Bread

Preparation time: 10 minutes. Cooking time: 25 minutes. Serving: 5

Ingredients:

- 2 cups of warm water tea
- 50g of fresh yeast or 1 small packet of dry granulated yeast (11 g)
- 4 tbsp oil soup
- 1 tsp salt tea
- 5 and ½ cups of wheat flour tea
- Oil or butter to grease.
- 100g sliced salami
- 200g grated mozzarella cheese
- 3 large tomatoes
- 1 tbsp oregano
- Salt and pepper to taste

Direction:

1. Mix the water, yeast, oil, salt, and flour. Divide the dough into 5 parts and let stand for 10 minutes on the surface greased with olive oil or butter and covered with a cloth.

2. Pass the tomatoes for food processor rummaging into slightly large pieces and season with salt, pepper, oregano, and reserve. Divide the ingredients fill in 5 parts and set aside. Preheat the air fryer. Set the time of 5 minutes and the temperature to 200°C.

3. Open each portion of dough with your hands leaving the center flatter and thicker, making the edge of the dough. Open in a size that fits in the basket of your air fryer. Place the dough, fix, but do not squeeze so that the dough does not enter the holes in the basket. Set the time of 10 minutes and the temperature to 180°C.

4. Once that time has passed, a little tomato sauce is poured into the center of the dough and the spread of the edges. Place the mozzarella cheese on top and slices of salami. Brush with butter or margarine on the edge of the pizza. Set another 5 to 10 minutes at 200°C and press the power button until the edges begin to brown.

Nutrition Value (Nutrition per Serving):

- Calories: 313
- Fat: 13.2 g
- Carbohydrates: 35.5g
- Proteins: 13.0g
- Sugar: 3.6g
- Cholesterol: 27.8mg

Curd Cheese with Milanese

Preparation time: 4 minutes. Cooking time: 10 minutes. Serving: 4-5

Ingredients:

- 400g diced curd cheese
- 3 whole eggs
- 300g of flour mixed with 1 tbsp of cornstarch
- 300g of breadcrumbs

Direction:

1. Place the breadcrumbs in a nonstick pot or skillet over medium heat, stirring all the time until it acquires a gold color, lightly toasted, this will give it a better look in the final result.

2. Cut the cheese into cubes. Involve the cheese cubes in the lightly beaten cut eggs, then in the mixture of wheat flour with corn starch, again in the eggs and finally in the breadcrumbs. Squeeze after the breadcrumbs. Spread the already breaded squares on a baking sheet and bring freezer for approximately two hours.

3. Preheat the air fryer. Set the time of 5 minutes and the temperature to 200°C.

4. Place the cheese cubes in the basket of the air fryer. Set the time to 5 minutes and press the power button. Shake the basket in half the time to get a more uniform result. At the end, transfer to a plate and serve next.

Nutrition Value (Nutrition per Serving):

- Calories: 90
- Fat: 7g
- Carbohydrates: 1g
- Protein: 6
- Sugar: 0g
- Cholesterol: 25mg

Cheese Bread

Preparation time: 10 minutes. Cooking time: 50 minutes. Serving: 30

Ingredients:

- 1kg cassava starch
- 1 tbsp of salt
- ½ cup of boiling water
- 250g margarine
- 4 eggs
- ½ liter of milk
- 250g of thick grated Minas cheese

Direction:

1. First, mix the salt with the flour in a bowl, and then gradually put the boiling water stirring constantly until all the water spills. Then add the eggs, margarine, and milk. When it is homogeneous add the grated cheese and knead well with hands until it stays uniform and begins to release from the hands.
2. Make balls around 4 cm with the dough and put on a baking sheet. Freeze for at least 30 minutes before baking.
3. Preheat the air fryer. Set the time of 5 minutes and the temperature to 200°C.
4. Place the cheese loaves in the basket of the air fryer leaving about 2 cm of each, as they will grow. Set the time of the air fryer to 15 minutes and press the power button. Shake the basket in half the time and if necessary, adjust the time.

Nutrition Value (Nutrition per Serving):

- Calories: 196
- Fat: 10g
- Carbohydrates: 21.5g
- Protein: 5g
- Sugar: 1g
- Cholesterol: 4.8mg

Homemade Pizzas

Preparation time: 5 minutes. Cooking time: 20 minutes. Serving: 4

Ingredients:

- 4 slices of bread
- 4 tbsp fresh Quark cheese
- Chopped chives
- Spinach leaves
- Rolled mushrooms
- 100g fresh goat cheese
- 25g of pine nuts
- Pepper
- Salt

Direction:

1. Spread each slice of sliced bread with a tablespoon of fresh Quark cheese.
2. Sprinkle with chopped chives and add some spinach leaves on top.
3. Clean the mushrooms and cut into thin slices, sprinkle with lemon juice to prevent them from blackening. Add the mushrooms to the pizzas. Add the pepper.
4. Add the goat cheese cut into small pieces and sprinkle the pine nuts.
5. Preheat the air fryer a few minutes to 200^0C.
6. Add the goat cheese cut into small pieces and sprinkle the pine nuts on top.
7. Set the timer of the air fryer from 7 to 10 minutes to 200^0C.

Nutrition Value (Nutrition per Serving):

- Calories: 236
- Fat: 5.2g
- Carbohydrates: 10g
- Protein: 7.8g
- Sugar: 0g
- Cholesterol: 33mg

Leek Quiche

Preparation time: 10. Cooking time: 20 minutes. Serving: 8

Ingredients:

- 4 Leeks well washed and cut
- 1 onion
- 1 terrine of 250g of fresh Quark cheese
- 4 tbsp grated cheese
- 4 eggs
- 2 tbsp olive oil
- Salt and pepper
- 1 mass of breeze pasta

Direction:

1. Wash the leeks and chop the white part.
2. Cut the onion and chop.
3. Poach the leeks together with the onion, in a pan with a little oil.
4. Season and cover, if all the oil is absorbed, add a little water and finish poaching. When we have leeks with onion ready, set aside.
5. Meanwhile, in a separate bowl, lay the eggs and beat, add the fresh cheese, and mix until you get a homogeneous cream. Then salt and add the grated cheese.
6. Arrange the breeze dough on a bowl and prick with a fork to prevent swelling. Deposit the poached vegetables on top, distributing them well and incorporate the preparation of the eggs and other ingredients. Cover with foil.
7. Preheat the air fryer a few minutes to 180^0C.
8. Place the container in the basket of the air fryer and set the timer for about 25 minutes at 180^0C.
9. If everything does not fit in the same container you can do it in two phases. Prick with a stick to verify that it has been cooked correctly.

Nutrition Value (Nutrition per Serving):

- Calories: 247
- Fat: 15g
- Carbohydrates: 23g
- Protein: 5g
- Sugar: 0mg
- Cholesterol: 0mg

Bags of Mushrooms Grown with Ham

Preparation time: 10 minutes. Cooking time: 10 minutes. Serving: 4

Ingredients:

- 150g of cultivated mushrooms
- 1 small brick of cream for cooking
- 100g of Serrano ham
- 230g of broken dough
- Salt
- Pepper

Direction:

1. Cut mushrooms and ham into small pieces. Then mix in a bowl with the cream and salt and pepper.
2. Divide and cut the broken dough into eight squares of 10 cm each. Fill the center of each square with a tablespoon of the previous mixture.
3. To close the bags, join each corner of the square towards the center, then prick the dough a little and paint with beaten egg.
4. Preheat the air fryer a few minutes to 200°C. Place the bags in the basket of the air fryer and set the timer for 15 minutes at a temperature of 200°C.

Nutrition Value (Nutrition per Serving):

- Calories: 264
- Fat: 8.56g
- Carbohydrates: 1.38g
- Protein: 6.77g
- Sugar: 0.47g
- Cholesterol: 0mg

Monkfish Skewers with Vegetables

Preparation time: 10 minutes. Cooking time: 20 minutes. Serving: 4

Ingredients:

- 400g monkfish
- 240g cherry tomatoes
- 1 zucchini
- 4 mushrooms
- 1 green pepper
- 1 tbsp olive oil
- Salt
- Chopsticks

Direction:

1. Mount the skewers interspersing cherry tomato, monkfish, zucchini, mushroom, pepper, until completing the stick or skewer as seen in the photo.
2. Preheat the air fryer a few minutes at 180°C.
3. Meanwhile, brush the skewers with a little oil.
4. Insert them in the basket and set the timer for about 5 minutes at 180°C.
5. Turn around when they are a little golden.
6. Finish browning and serving.

Nutrition Value (Nutrition per Serving):

- Calories: 65
- Fat: 0.5g
- Carbohydrates: 0g
- Protein: 14.8g

Hamburger with French Fries

Preparation time: 5 minutes. Cooking time: 200 minutes. Serving: 4

Ingredients:

- 4 hamburger bread rolls
- 1 fresh tomato
- Lettuce leaves (amount needed)
- 250g Minced meat
- 1 beaten egg
- 600g potatoes
- Oregano
- Chopped garlic
- Chopped onion
- Salt
- Pepper
- Mustard

Direction:

1. Peel and cut the potatoes. Go through water and dry very well. Put in a bowl and sprinkle with oil.
2. Preheat the air fryer a few minutes at 200^0C.
3. Put the potatoes in the basket of the air fryer and set the timer 20 minutes to 200°C. When ready add salt and reserve.
4. Apart mix the minced meat with oregano, chopped garlic, mustard, chopped onion and beaten egg. Form four meatballs and shape each of them hamburger.
5. Preheat the air fryer for a few minutes at 180^0 C. Place the burgers in the basket and set the timer for about 10 minutes at 180^0C.
6. Prepare each muffin with some tomato slices, some lettuce leaves and some onion slices. Then incorporate the hamburger and close the bun.
7. Serve with French fries

Nutrition Value (Nutrition per Serving):

- Calories: 297
- Fat: 13g
- Carbohydrates: 39.6
- Protein: 3.9
- Sugar: 0.1g
- Cholesterol: 40mg

Egg to The Plate

Preparation time: 5 minutes. Cooking time: 25 minutes. Serve: 1

Ingredients:

- 2 eggs
- 1 tbsp tomato sauce
- 1 good handful of frozen peas
- 1 slice of sliced sovory1 dash of olive oil
- Salt and pepper

Direction:

1. Preheat the air fryer about 3 minutes at 180^0C.
2. Lightly brush the clay pot with the oil.
3. Spread the tomato sauce on the base of the casserole and place the peas on top.
4. Shell the two eggs and place them carefully on the bed of peas.
5. Spread the pieces of savory around the eggs and salt and pepper to taste.
6. Put the casserole in the basket, close and set the timer for about 12 minutes at 180^0C.
7. Remove the casserole very carefully so as not to burn and serve in the same container.

Nutrition Value (Nutrition per Serving):

- Calories: 787
- Fat: 10.28g
- Carbohydrates: 9.96g
- Protein: 14.21g
- Sugar: 5.93g
- Cholesterol: 423mg

Crashed Bones with Chips and Ham

Preparation time: 5 minutes. Cooking time: 20 minutes. Serve: 4

Ingredients:

- 600g potatoes
- Salt
- 1 tbsp olive oil
- 100g of Iberian Ham
- 4 eggs

Direction:

1. Cut the elongated French fries, go through plenty of water and dry well with paper towels.
2. Spray with oil and preheat the air fryer a few minutes at 200°C.
3. Place the potatoes in the basket of the air fryer and set the timer for 25 minutes at 200°C.
4. When we see that they are starting to brown, put paper under the potatoes and lay the eggs.
5. Put in the air fryer again 5 more minutes.
6. Finally add Iberian ham flakes.
7. If you want to go faster while the potatoes are fried in the air fryer you can prepare the grilled eggs in a small pan and then mix with the potatoes and ham on the plate.

Nutrition Value (Nutrition per Serving):

- Calories: 162.6
- Fat: 12g
- Carbohydrates: 0.6g
- Protein: 16.6g
- Glycemic Index: 0

Chapter 4: Poultry

Turkey and Cream Cheese Breast Pillows

Preparation time: 5 minutes. Cooking time: 10 minutes. Serving: 45

Ingredients:

- 1 cup of milk with 1 egg inside (put the egg in the cup and then fill with milk)
- 1/3 cup of water
- ¼ cup olive oil or oil
- 1 and ¾ teaspoon of salt
- 2 tbsp sugar
- 2 and ½ tbsp dried granular yeast
- 4 cups of flour
- 1 egg yolk to brush
- 2 jars of cream cheese
- 15 slices of turkey breast cut in 4

Direction:

1. Mix all the dough ingredients with your hands until it is very smooth. After the ready dough, make small balls and place on a floured surface. Reserve
2. Open each dough ball with a roller trying to make it square. Cut squares of approximately 10 X 10 cm. Fill with a piece of turkey breast and 1 teaspoon of cream cheese coffee. Close the union of the masses joining the 4 points. Brush with the egg yolk and set aside.
3. Preheat the air fryer. Set the timer of 5 minutes and the temperature to 200C.
4. Place 6 units in the basket of the air fryer and bake for 4 or 5 minutes at 180C. Repeat until all the pillows have finished cooking.

Nutrition Value (Nutrition per Serving):

- Calories: 538
- Fat: 29.97g
- Carbohydrates: 22.69g
- Protein: 43.64g
- Sugar: 0.56g
- Cholesterol: 137mg

Chicken Wings

Preparation time: 10 minutes. Cooking time: 25 minutes. Serve: 2

Ingredients:

- 10 chicken wings (about 700g)
- Oil in spay
- 1 tbsp soy sauce
- ½ tbsp cornstarch
- 2 tbsp honey
- 1 tbsp ground fresh chili paste
- 1 tbsp minced garlic
- ½ tsp chopped fresh ginger
- 1 tbsp lime sumo
- ½ tbsp salt
- 2 tbsp chives

Direction:

1. Dry the chicken with a tea towel. Cover the chicken with the oil spray.
2. Place the chicken inside the hot air electric fryer, separating the wings towards the edge so that it is not on top of each other. Cook at 200°C until the skin is crispy for about 25 min. Turn them around half the time.
3. Mix the soy sauce with cornstarch in a small pan. Add honey, chili paste, garlic, ginger, and lime sumo. Simmer until it boils and thickens. Place the chicken in a bowl, add the sauce and cover all the chicken. Sprinkle with chives.

Nutrition Value (Nutrition per Serving):

- Calories: 81
- Fat: 5.4g
- Carbohydrates: 0g
- Protein: 7.46g
- Sugar: 0g
- Cholesterol: 23mg

Pickled Poultry

Preparation time: 10 minutes. Cooking time: 25 minutes. Serve: 4

Ingredients:

- 600g of poultry, without bones or skin
- 3 white onions, peeled and cut into thin slices
- 5 garlic cloves, peeled and sliced
- 3 dl olive oil
- 1 dl apple cider vinegar
- ½ l white wine
- 2 bay leaves
- 5 g peppercorns
- Flour
- Pepper
- Salt

Direction:

1. Rub the bird in dice that we will pepper and flour
2. Put a pan with oil on the fire. When the oil is hot, fry the floured meat dice in it until golden brown. Take them out and reserve, placing them in a clay or oven dish. Strain the oil in which you have fried the meat
3. Preheat the oven to 170° C
4. Put the already cast oil in another pan over the fire. Sauté the garlic and onions in it. Add the white wine and let cook about 3 minutes. Remove the pan from the heat, add the vinegar to the oil and wine. Remove, rectify salt, and pour this mixture into the source where you had left the bird dice. Introduce the source in the oven, lower the temperature to 140°C and bake for 1 and ½ hours. Remove the source from the oven and let it stand at room temperature
5. When the source is cold, put it in the fridge and let it rest a few hours before serving.

Nutrition Value (Nutrition per Serving):

- Calories: 232
- Fat: 15g
- Carbohydrates: 5.89g
- Protein: 18.2g
- Sugar: 1.72g
- Cholesterol: 141mg

Cordon Bleu Chicken Breast

Preparation time: 10 minutes. Cooking time: 40 minutes. Serve: 6

Ingredients:

- 4 flattened chicken breasts
- 8 slices of ham
- 16 slices of Swiss cheese
- 2 tsp fresh thyme
- ¼ cup flour
- 1 cup of ground bread
- 2 tsp melted butter
- 2 eggs
- 1 clove garlic finely chopped
- pam cooking spray

Direction:

1. Preheat the air fryer to 350 degrees Fahrenheit (180 °C), set timer to 5 minutes. Then, flatten chicken breasts.
2. Fill the chicken breasts with two slices of cheese, then 2 slices of ham and finally 2 slices of cheese and roll up. Use a stick if necessary, to save the shape.
3. Mix the ground bread with the thyme, the garlic finely chopped, with the melted butter and with salt and pepper. Beat the eggs. Season the flour with salt and pepper.
4. Pass the chicken rolls first through the flour, then through the egg and finally through the breadcrumbs.
5. Bake until the breasts are cooked, about 20 minutes.
6. Alternatively, before putting the chicken breasts in the air fryer you can fry them in a little butter and then finish cooking in the air fryer for 13-15 minutes.

Nutrition Value (Nutrition per Serving):

- Calories: 387
- Fat: 20g
- Carbohydrates: 18g
- Protein: 33g
- Sugar: 0g
- Cholesterol: 42mg

Fried Chicken

Preparation time: 15 minutes. Cooking time: 25 minutes. Serve: 4

Ingredients:

- 1kg of chicken chopped into small pieces
- Garlic powder
- Salt
- Ground pepper
- 1 little grated ginger
- 1 lemon
- Extra virgin olive oil

Direction:

1. Put the chicken in a large bowl.
2. Add the lemon juice and pepper.
3. Add some grated ginger and mix well.
4. Leave 15 minutes in the refrigerator.
5. Add now a jet of extra virgin olive oil and mix.
6. Put the chicken in the air fryer, if it does not fit in a batch, it is put in two.
7. Select 180 degrees, 25 minutes.
8. Shake the baskets a few times so that the chicken rotates and is made on all sides.
9. If you want to pass the chicken for flour, before putting it in the basket and frying, you can do it.

Nutrition Value (Nutrition per Serving):

- Calories: 4
- Fat: 3.3g
- Carbohydrates: 2.3g
- Protein: 2.5g
- Sugar: 0.1g
- Cholesterol: 8.8mg

Rolls Stuffed with Broccoli and Carrots with Chicken

Preparation time: 15 minutes. Cooking time: 25 minutes. Serve: 4

Ingredients:

- 8 sheets of rice pasta
- 1 chicken breast
- 1 onion
- 1 carrot
- 150g broccolis
- 1 can of sweet corn
- Extra virgin olive oil
- Salt
- Ground pepper
- Soy sauce
- 1 bag of rice three delicacies

Direction:

1. Start with the vegetable that you have to cook previously, stop them, peel the carrot.
2. Cut the carrot and broccoli as small as you can. Add the broccolis and the carrot to a pot with boiling water and let cook a few minutes, they have to be tender, but not too much, that crunch a little.
3. Drain well and reserve.
4. Cut the onion into julienne.
5. Cut the breast into strips.
6. In the Wok, put some extra virgin olive oil.
7. Add to the wok when it is hot, the onion and the chicken breast.
8. Sauté well until the chicken is cooked.
9. Drain the corn and add to the wok along with the broccolis and the carrot.
10. Sauté so that the ingredients are mixed.
11. Add salt, ground pepper and a little soy sauce.
12. Mix well and let the filling cool.
13. Hydrate the rice pasta sheets.

14. Spread on the worktable and distribute the filling between the sheets of rice paste.

15. Assemble the rolls and paint with a little oil.

16. Put in the air fryer, those who enter do not pile up.

17. Select 10 minutes 200 degrees.

18. When you have all the rolls made, the first ones will have cooled, because to solve it, you now place all the rolls already cooked inside the air fryer, now it does not matter that they are piled up.

19. Select 180 degrees, 5 minutes.

20. Make while the rice as indicated by the manufacturer in its bag.

21. Serve the rice with the rolls.

Nutrition Value (Nutrition per Serving):

- Calories: 125
- Fat: 4.58g
- Carbohydrates: 16.83g
- Protein: 4.69g
- Sugar: 4.43g
- Cholesterol: 0mg

Chicken Flutes with Sour Sauce and Guacamole

Preparation time: 15 minutes. Cooking time: 25 minutes. Serve: 4

Ingredients:

- 8 wheat cakes
- 1 large roasted breast
- Grated cheese
- Sour sauce
- Guacamole
- Extra virgin olive oil

Direction:

1. Extend the wheat cakes.
2. Stuffed with grated cheese and well-roasted chicken breast.
3. Form the flues and paint with extra virgin olive oil.
4. Place in batches in the air fryer and select 180 degrees, 5 minutes on each side or until you see the flutes golden.
5. Serve with sour sauce and guacamole.

Nutrition Value (Nutrition per Serving):

- Calories: 325
- Fat: 7g
- Carbohydrates: 45g
- Protein: 13g
- Sugar: 7g
- Cholesterol: 0mg

Spicy Chicken Strips

Preparation time: 5 minutes. Cooking time: 12 minutes. Serve: 5

Ingredients:

- 1 cup buttermilk
- 1½ tbsp hot pepper sauce
- 1 tsp salt
- ½ tsp black pepper, divided
- 1 pound boneless and skinless chicken breasts, cut into ¾ inch strips
- ¾ cup panko breadcrumbs
- ½ tsp salt
- ¼ tsp hot pepper, or to taste
- 1 tbsp olive oil

Direction:

1. Put the buttermilk, hot sauce, salt and ¼ teaspoon of black pepper in shallow bowl. Add chicken strips and refrigerate for at least two hours. Put breadcrumbs, salt, and the remaining black pepper and hot pepper in another bowl; Add and stir the oil.
2. Remove the chicken strips from the marinade and discard the marinade. Put the strips, few at the same time, to the crumb mixture. Press the crumbs to the strips to achieve a uniform and firm cover.
3. Put half of the strips in single layer inside the basket. Cook at a temperature of 350°F for 12 minutes. Cook the rest when the first batch is cooked.

Nutrition Value (Nutrition per Serving):

- Calories: 207
- Fat: 9g
- Carbohydrates: 5g
- Protein: 25g
- Sugar: 0g
- Cholesterol: 0mg

Chicken Breasts Covered With Parmesan Cheese

Preparation time: 5 minutes. Cooking time: 12 minutes. Serve: 2

Ingredients:

- ¼ cup panko breadcrumbs
- ¼ cup grated Parmesan cheese
- ¼ tsp dried basil
- 1 tbsp olive oil
- 1 tbsp spicy mustard
- 1 tsp Worcestershire sauce
- 2 boneless and skinless chicken breasts

Direction:

1. Put the breadcrumbs, cheese, and basil in a small, shallow bowl. Add and stir the oil until completely mixed. Combine mustard with Worcestershire sauce in small bowl. Put the mustard mixture on both sides of the breasts.

2. Put the chicken in the bowl with the crumb mixture and press the crumbs on both sides of the breasts to achieve a uniform and firm cover.

3. Put the chicken inside the basket. Cook at a temperature of 350°F for 21 to 25 minutes, turning halfway through cooking.

Nutrition Value (Nutrition per Serving):

- Calories: 386
- Fat: 10g
- Carbohydrates: 5g
- Proteins: 29g
- Sugar: 0g
- Cholesterol: 73mg

Chicken In Wheat Cake With Aioli Sauce

Preparation time: 10 minutes. Cooking time: 35 minutes. Serve: 4

Ingredients:

- 500g breaded chicken
- 4 wheat cakes
- Extra virgin olive oil
- 1 small lettuce
- Grated cheese
- Aioli sauce

Direction:

1. Put the breaded chicken in the air fryer with a little extra virgin olive oil and fry at 180 degrees for 20 minutes.
2. Take out and reserve.
3. Chop the lettuce,
4. Put the wheat cakes on the worktable and distribute the chopped lettuce between them.
5. On the chopped lettuce spread the pieces of breaded chicken.
6. Cover with grated cheese and add some aioli sauce.
7. Close the wheat cakes and place on the baking sheet.
8. Take to the oven, 180 degrees, 15 minutes or until the cheese is melted.

Nutrition Value (Nutrition per Serving):

- Calories: 91
- Fat: 9.83g
- Carbohydrates: 1.06g
- Protein: 0.19g
- Sugar: 0.07g
- Cholesterol: 0mg

Soy Chicken and Sesame, Breaded and Fried

Preparation time: 10 minutes. Cooking time: 50 minutes. Serve: 4

Ingredients:

- 1 large chicken breast
- Egg
- Breadcrumbs
- Extra virgin olive oil
- Salt
- Ground pepper
- Soy sauce
- Sesame

Direction:

1. Cut the breast into fillets and put in a bowl.
2. Season.
3. Add soy sauce and sesame. Flirt well and leave 30 minutes.
4. Beat the eggs and pass all the steaks through the beaten egg and the breadcrumbs.
5. With a silicone brush, permeate the fillets well on both sides.
6. Place on the grill of the air fryer and select 180 degrees, 20 minutes.
7. Make the fillets in batches so that they pile against each other.

Nutrition Value (Nutrition per Serving):

- Calories: 373
- Fat: 18.30g
- Carbohydrates: 6.24g
- Proteins: 34.74g
- Sugars: 5.67g
- Cholesterol: 0 mg

Chicken with Provencal Herbs and Potatoes

Preparation time: 10 minutes. Cooking time: 55 minutes. Serve: 2

Ingredients:

- 4 potatoes
- 2 chicken hindquarters
- Provencal herbs
- Salt
- Ground pepper
- Extra virgin olive oil

Direction:

1. Peel the potatoes and cut into slices.
2. Pepper and put on the grid of the base air fryer.
3. Impregnate the chicken well with oil, salt and pepper and put some Provencal herbs.
4. Place the chicken on the potatoes.
5. Take the grill to the bucket of the air fryer and put inside.
6. Select 170 degrees 40 minutes.
7. Turn the chicken and leave 15 more minutes.

Nutrition Value (Nutrition per Serving):

- Calories: 198.5
- Fat: 4.2g
- Carbohydrates: 17.6g
- Protein: 21.7g
- Sugar: 0.82g

Chicken Tears

Preparation time: 15 minutes. Cooking time: 25 minutes. Serve: 4

Ingredients:

- 2 chicken breasts
- Flour
- Salt
- Ground pepper
- Extra virgin olive oil
- Lemon juice
- Garlic powder

Direction:

1. Cut the chicken breasts into tears. Season and put some lemon juice and garlic powder. Let flirt well.
2. Go through flour and shake.
3. Place the tears in the basket of the air fryer and paint with extra virgin olive oil.
4. Select 180 degrees, 20 minutes.
5. Move from time to time so that the tears are made on all their faces.

Nutrition Value (Nutrition per Serving):

- Calories: 197
- Fat: 8g
- Carbohydrates: 16g
- Protein: 14g
- Sugar: 0mg
- Cholesterol: 0mg

Breaded Chicken with Seed Chips

Preparation time: 10 minutes. Cooking time: 40 minutes. Serve: 4

Ingredients:

- 12 chicken breast fillets
- Salt
- 2 eggs
- 1 small bag of seed chips
- Breadcrumbs
- Extra virgin olive oil

Direction:

1. Put salt to chicken fillets.
2. Crush the seed chips and when we have them fine, bind with the breadcrumbs.
3. Beat the two eggs.
4. Pass the chicken breast fillets through the beaten egg and then through the seed chips that you have tied with the breadcrumbs.
5. When you have them all breaded, paint with a brush of extra virgin olive oil.
6. Place the fillets in the basket of the air fryer without being piled up.
7. Select 170 degrees, 20 minutes.
8. Take out and put another batch, repeat temperature and time. So, until you use up all the steaks.

Nutrition Value (Nutrition per Serving):

- Calories: 242
- Fat: 13g
- Carbohydrates: 13.5g
- Protein: 18g
- Sugar: 0g
- Cholesterol: 42mg

Salted Biscuit Pie Turkey Chops

Preparation time: 5 minutes. Cooking time: 20 minutes. Serve: 4

Ingredients:

- 8 large turkey chops
- 300 gr of crackers
- 2 eggs
- Extra virgin olive oil
- Salt
- Ground pepper

Direction:

1. Put the turkey chops on the worktable, and salt and pepper.
2. Beat the eggs in a bowl.
3. Crush the cookies in the Thermomix with a few turbo strokes until they are made grit, or you can crush them with the blender.
4. Put the cookies in a bowl.
5. Pass the chops through the beaten egg and then passed them through the crushed cookies. Press well so that the empanada is perfect.
6. Paint the empanada with a silicone brush and extra virgin olive oil.
7. Put the chops in the basket of the air fryer, not all will enter. They will be done in batches.
8. Select 200 degrees, 15 minutes.
9. When you have all the chops made, serve.

Nutrition Value (Nutrition per Serving):

- Calories: 126
- Fat: 6g
- Carbohydrates 0g
- Protein: 18g
- Sugar: 0g
- Cholesterol: 0mg

Lemon Chicken with Basil

Preparation time: 10 minutes. Cooking time: 1h. Serve: 4

Ingredients:

- 1kg chopped chicken
- 1 or 2 lemons
- Basil, salt, and ground pepper
- Extra virgin olive oil

Direction:

1. Put the chicken in a bowl with a jet of extra virgin olive oil.
2. Put salt, pepper, and basil.
3. Bind well and let stand for at least 30 minutes stirring occasionally.
4. Put the pieces of chicken in the air fryer basket and take the air fryer
5. Select 30 minutes.
6. Occasionally remove.
7. Take out and put another batch.
8. Do the same operation.

Nutrition Value (Nutrition per Serving):

- Calories: 1,440
- Fat: 74.9g
- Carbohydrates: 122.0g
- Protein: 68.6g
- Sugar: 55.2g
- Cholesterol: 203.8mg

Fried Chicken Tamari and Mustard

Preparation time: 15 minutes. Cooking time: 1h 20 minutes. Serve: 4

Ingredients:

- 1kg of very small chopped chicken
- Tamari Sauce
- Original mustard
- Ground pepper
- 1 lemon
- Flour
- Extra virgin olive oil

Direction:

1. Put the chicken in a bowl, you can put the chicken with or without the skin, to everyone's taste.
2. Add a generous stream of tamari, one or two tablespoons of mustard, a little ground pepper and a splash of lemon juice.
3. Link everything very well and let macerate an hour.
4. Pass the chicken pieces for flour and place in the air fryer basket.
5. Put 20 minutes at 200 degrees. At half time, move the chicken from the basket.
6. Do not crush the chicken, it is preferable to make two or three batches of chicken to pile up and do not fry the pieces well.

Nutrition Value (Nutrition per Serving):

- Calories: 100
- Fat: 5g
- Carbohydrates: 5g
- Protein: 8g
- Sugar: 0g
- Cholesterol: 5mg

Breaded Chicken Fillets

Preparation time: 10 minutes. Cooking time: 25 minutes. Serve: 4

Ingredients:

- 3 small chicken breasts or 2 large chicken breasts
- Salt
- Ground pepper
- 3 garlic cloves
- 1 lemon
- Beaten eggs
- Breadcrumbs
- Extra virgin olive oil

Direction:

1. Cut the breasts into fillets.
2. Put in a bowl and add the lemon juice, chopped garlic cloves and pepper.
3. Flirt well and leave 10 minutes.
4. Beat the eggs and put breadcrumbs on another plate.
5. Pass the chicken breast fillets through the beaten egg and the breadcrumbs.
6. When you have them all breaded, start to fry.
7. Paint the breaded breasts with a silicone brush and extra virgin olive oil.
8. Place a batch of fillets in the basket of the air fryer and select 10 minutes 180 degrees.
9. Turn around and leave another 5 minutes at 180 degrees.

Nutrition Value (Nutrition per Serving):

- Calories: 120
- Fat: 14g
- Carbohydrates: 10g
- Protein: 17g
- Sugar: 0g
- Cholesterol: 60mg

Dry Rub Chicken Wings

Preparation time: 5 minutes. Cooking time: 30 minutes. Serve: 4

Ingredients:

- 9g garlic powder
- 1 cube of chicken broth, reduced sodium
- 5g of salt
- 3g black pepper
- 1g smoked paprika
- 1g cayenne pepper
- 3g Old Bay seasoning, sodium free
- 3g onion powder
- 1g dried oregano
- 453g chicken wings
- Nonstick Spray Oil
- Ranch sauce, to serve

Direction:

1. Preheat the air fryer. Set the temperature to 180 °C.
2. Put ingredients in a bowl and mix well.
3. Season the chicken wings with half the seasoning mixture and sprinkle abundantly with oil spray.
4. Place the chicken wings in the preheated air fryer.
5. Select Chicken, set the timer to 30 minutes.
6. Shake the baskets halfway through cooking.
7. Transfer the chicken wings to a bowl and sprinkle them with the other half of the seasonings until they are well covered. Serve with ranch sauce

Nutrition Value (Nutrition per Serving):

- Calories: 89
- Fat: 6.33g
- Carbohydrates: 0g
- Protein: 7.56g
- Sugar: 0g
- Cholesterol: 0mg

Mongolian Chicken Wings

Preparation time: 15 minutes. Cooking time: 35 minutes. Serve: 2-4

Ingredients:

- 680g chicken wings
- 30 ml of vegetable oil
- Salt and pepper to taste
- 60 ml of low sodium soy sauce
- 85g honey
- 20 ml rice wine vinegar
- 15g Sriracha sauce
- 3 cloves garlic, minced
- 4g fresh ginger, grated
- 1 chopped green onion to decorate

Direction:

1. Select Preheat, set the temperature to 180°C and press Start / Pause.
2. Mix chicken wings with oil, salt, and pepper until well coated.
3. Place the covered chicken wings in the preheated air fryer.
4. Select Chicken and press Start/Pause.
5. Put soy sauce, honey, rice wine vinegar, Sriracha, garlic and ginger in a saucepan.
6. Cook over low heat until the flavors come together, and the glaze is slightly reduced, approximately for 10 minutes.
7. Transfer the chicken wings, after 20 minutes, to a large bowl and mix them with the glaze.
8. Return the chicken wings to the fryer baskets and cook for 5 more minutes.
9. Garnish with green onions and serve.

Nutrition Value (Nutrition per Serving):

- Energy: 4360
- Fat: 24.69g
- Carbohydrates: 148.31g
- Protein: 67.04g
- Sugar: 12.34g
- Cholesterol: 183mg

Chicken Wings with Sriracha And Honey

Preparation time: 5 minutes. Cooking time: 30 minutes. Serve: 2-4

Ingredients:

- 2g smoked paprika
- 2g garlic powder
- 2g onion powder
- 2g of salt
- 2g black pepper
- 25g cornstarch
- 453g chicken wings
- Nonstick Spray Oil
- 90g of honey
- 100g Sriracha sauce
- 15 ml rice wine vinegar
- 5 ml sesame oil

Direction:

1. Preheat the air fryer, set the temperature to 195 °C.
2. Mix smoked paprika, garlic powder, onion powder, salt, black pepper, and corn.
3. Mix the wings in the seasoned cornstarch until they are covered evenly.
4. Spray the wings with aerosol oil and mix them until they are covered with oil.
5. Place the wings in the preheated air fryer.
6. Select Chicken, set the timer to 30 minutes and press Start / Pause.
7. Shake the baskets halfway through cooking.
8. Mix honey, Sriracha, rice wine vinegar and sesame oil in a large bowl.
9. Mix the cooked wings in the sauce until they are well covered and serve.

Nutrition Value (Nutrition per Serving):

- Calories: 185
- Fat: 5g
- Carbohydrates: 9g
- Protein: 26g

Chicken Wings with Garlic Parmesan

Preparation time: 5 minutes. Cooking time: 25 minutes. Serve: 3

Ingredients:

- 25g cornstarch
- 20g grated Parmesan cheese
- 9g garlic powder
- Salt and pepper to taste
- 680g chicken wings
- Nonstick Spray Oil

Direction:

1. Select Preheat, set the temperature to 200 °C and press Start / Pause.
2. Combine corn starch, Parmesan, garlic powder, salt, and pepper in a bowl.
3. Mix the chicken wings in the seasoning and dip until well coated.
4. Spray the baskets and the air fryer with oil spray and add the wings, sprinkling the tops of the wings as well.
5. Select Chicken and press Start/Pause. Be sure to shake the baskets in the middle of cooking.
6. Sprinkle with what's left of the Parmesan mix and serve.

Nutrition Value (Nutrition per Serving):

- Calories: 204
- Fat: 15g
- Carbohydrates: 1g
- Proteins: 12g
- Sugar: 0g
- Cholesterol: 63mg

Jerk Style Chicken Wings

Preparation time: 5 minutes. Cooking time: 25 minutes. Serve: 2-3

Ingredients:

- 1g ground thyme
- 1g dried rosemary
- 2g allspice
- 4g ground ginger
- 3 g garlic powder
- 2g onion powder
- 1g of cinnamon
- 2g of paprika
- 2g chili powder
- 1g nutmeg
- Salt to taste
- 30 ml of vegetable oil
- 0.5 - 1 kg of chicken wings
- 1 lime, juice

Direction:

1. Select Preheat, set the temperature to 200°C and press Start/Pause.
2. Combine all spices and oil in a bowl to create a marinade.
3. Mix the chicken wings in the marinade until they are well covered.
4. Place the chicken wings in the preheated air fryer.
5. Select Chicken and press Start/Pause. Be sure to shake the baskets in the middle of cooking.
6. Remove the wings and place them on a serving plate.
7. Squeeze fresh lemon juice over the wings and serve.

Nutrition Value (Nutrition per Serving):

- Calories: 240
- Fat: 15g
- Carbohydrate: 5g
- Protein: 19g
- Sugars: 4g
- Cholesterol: 60mg

Chicken Skewers with Garlic and Herb

Preparation time: 5 minutes. Cooking time: 10 minutes. Serve: 2-4

Ingredients:

- 60 ml of olive oil
- 3 cloves garlic, grated
- 2g dried oregano
- 1g dried thyme
- 2g of salt
- 1g black pepper
- 1 lemon, juice
- 454g chicken thighs, boneless, skinless, cut into 38 mm pieces
- 2 wooden skewers, cut in half

Direction:

1. Mix olive oil, garlic, oregano, thyme, salt, black pepper, and lemon juice in a large bowl.
2. Add the chicken to the marinade and marinate for 1 hour.
3. Select Preheat, set the temperature to 195 °C and press Start / Pause.
4. Cut the marinated chicken into 38 mm pieces and spread it on the skewers.
5. Place the skewers in the preheated air fryer.
6. Select Chicken, set the time to 10 minutes and press Start/Pause.

Nutrition Value (Nutrition per Serving):

- Calories: 215
- Fat: 13g
- Carbohydrates: 1g
- Protein: 22g
- Sugar: 1g
- Cholesterol: 130mg

Chicken Skewers with Yogurt

Preparation time: 4h 10 minutes. Cooking time: 10 minutes. Serve: 2-4

Ingredients:

- 123g of plain whole milk Greek yogurt
- 20 ml of olive oil
- 2g of paprika
- 1g cumin
- 1g crushed red pepper
- 1 lemon, juice and zest of the peel
- 5g of salt
- 1g freshly ground black pepper
- 4 cloves garlic, minced
- 454g chicken thighs, boneless, skinless, cut into 38 mm pieces
- 2 wooden skewers, cut in half
- Nonstick Spray Oil

Direction:

1. Mix the yogurt, olive oil, paprika, cumin, red paprika, lemon juice, lemon zest, salt, pepper, and garlic in a large bowl.
2. Add the chicken to the marinade and marinate in the fridge for at least 4 hours.
3. Select Preheat and press Start/Pause.
4. Cut the marinated chicken thighs into 38 mm pieces and spread them on skewers.
5. Place the skewers in the preheated air fryer.
6. Cook at 200°C for 10 minutes.

- Calories: 113
- Fat: 3.4g
- Carbohydrates: 0g
- Protein: 20.6g

Fried Lemon Chicken

Preparation time: 5 minutes. Cooking time: 20 minutes. Serve: 6

Ingredients:

- 6 chicken thighs
- 2 tbsp olive oil
- 2 tbsp lemon juice
- 1 tbsp Italian herbal seasoning mix
- 1 tsp Celtic sea salt
- 1 tsp ground fresh pepper
- 1 lemon, thinly sliced

Direction:

1. Add all ingredients, except sliced lemon, to bowl or bag, stir to cover chicken.
2. Let marinate for 30 minutes overnight.
3. Remove the chicken and let the excess oil drip (it doesn't need to dry out, just don't drip with tons of excess oil).
4. Arrange the chicken thighs and the lemon slices in the fryer basket, being careful not to push the chicken thighs too close to each other.
5. Set the fryer to 200 degrees and cook for 10 minutes.
6. Remove the basket from the fryer and turn the chicken thighs to the other side.
7. Cook again at 200 for another 10 minutes.
8. The chicken thighs will be crispy, with clear juices and will reach 165 degrees of internal temperature when checked with a digital thermometer inserted in the thickest part of the thigh.

- Calories: 215
- Fat: 13g
- Carbohydrates: 1g
- Protein: 22g
- Sugar: 1g
- Cholesterol: 130mg

Chicken's liver

Preparation time: 10 minutes. Cooking time: 30 minutes. Serve: 4

Ingredients:

- 500g of chicken livers
- 2 or 3 carrots
- 1 green pepper
- 1 red pepper
- 1 onion
- 4 tomatoes
- Salt
- Ground pepper
- 1 glass of white wine
- ½ glass of water
- Extra virgin olive oil

Direction:

1. Peel the carrots, cut them into slices and add them to the bowl of the air fryer with a tablespoon of extra virgin olive oil 5 minutes.
2. After 5 minutes add the peppers and onion in julienne. Select 5 minutes.
3. After that time, add the tomatoes in wedges and select 5 more minutes.
4. Add now the chicken liver clean and chopped.
5. Season, add the wine and water.
6. Select 10 minutes.
7. Check that the liver is tender.

Nutrition Value (Nutrition per Serving):

- Calories: 76
- Fat: 2.8g
- Carbohydrates: 0.5g
- Protein: 11.3g
- Sugar: 0g
- Cholesterol: 248.2mg

Chicken Thighs

Preparation time: 10 minutes. Cooking time: 20 minutes. Serve: 2

Ingredients:

- 4 chicken thighs
- Salt to taste
- Pepper
- Mustard
- Paprika

Direction:

1. Before using the pot, it is convenient to turn on for 5 minutes to heat it. Marinate the thighs with salt, pepper, mustard and paprika. Put your thighs in the air fryer for 10 minutes at 380^0F
2. After the time, turn the thighs and fry for 10 more minutes. If necessary, you can use an additional 5 minutes depending on the size of the thighs so that they are well cooked

Nutrition Value (Nutrition per Serving):

- Calories: 72
- Fat: 2.36g
- Carbohydrate: 0g
- Protein: 11.78g
- Sugar: 0g
- Cholesterol: 39

Chapter 5: Beef, Pork, Lamb Recipes

Mediterranean Lamb Meatballs

Preparation time: 10 minutes. Cooking time: 40 minutes. Serve: 4

Ingredients:

- 454g ground lamb
- 3 cloves garlic, minced
- 5g of salt
- 1g black pepper
- 2g of mint, freshly chopped
- 2g ground cumin
- 3 ml hot sauce
- 1g chili powder
- 1 scallion, chopped
- 8g parsley, finely chopped
- 15 ml of fresh lemon juice
- 2g lemon zest
- 10 ml of olive oil

Direction:

1. Mix the lamb, garlic, salt, pepper, mint, cumin, hot sauce, chili powder, chives, parsley, lemon juice and lemon zest until well combined.
2. Create balls with the lamb mixture and cool for 30 minutes.
3. Select Preheat in the air fryer and press Start/Pause.
4. Cover the meatballs with olive oil and place them in the preheated fryer.
5. Select Steak, set the time to 10 minutes and press Start/Pause.

Nutritional Value (Nutrition per Serving):

- Calories: 282
- Fat: 23.41
- Carbohydrates: 0g
- Protein: 16.59
- Sugar: 0g
- Cholesterol: 73gm

Pork Rind

Preparation time: 10 minutes. Cooking time: 1h. Serve: 4

Ingredients:

- 1kg of pork rinds
- Salt
- ½ tsp black pepper coffee

Direction:

- Preheat the air fryer. Set the time of 5 minutes and the temperature to 200^0C.
- Cut the bacon into cubes - 1 finger wide.
- Season with salt and a pinch of pepper.
- Place in the basket of the air fryer. Set the time of 45 minutes and press the power button.
- Shake the basket every 10 minutes so that the pork rinds stay golden brown equally.
- Once they are ready, drain a little on the paper towel so they stay dry. Transfer to a plate and serve.

Nutrition Value (Nutrition per Serving):

- Calories: 172
- Fat: 10.02g
- Carbohydrates: 0g
- Protein: 19.62g
- Sugar: 0g
- Cholesterol: 30 mg

Pork Trinoza Wrapped in Ham

Preparation time: 10 minutes. Cooking time: 20 minutes. Serve: 6

Ingredients:

- 6 pieces of Serrano ham, thinly sliced
- 454g pork, halved, with butter and crushed
- 6g of salt
- 1g black pepper
- 227g fresh spinach leaves, divided
- 4 slices of mozzarella cheese, divided
- 18g sun-dried tomatoes, divided
- 10 ml of olive oil, divided

Direction:

1. Place 3 pieces of ham on baking paper, slightly overlapping each other. Place 1 half of the pork in the ham. Repeat with the other half.
2. Season the inside of the pork rolls with salt and pepper.
3. Place half of the spinach, cheese, and sun-dried tomatoes on top of the pork loin, leaving a 13 mm border on all sides.
4. Roll the fillet around the filling well and tie with a kitchen cord to keep it closed.
5. Repeat the process for the other pork steak and place them in the fridge.
6. Select Preheat in the air fryer and press Start/Pause.
7. Brush 5 ml of olive oil on each wrapped steak and place them in the preheated air fryer.
8. Select Steak. Set the timer to 9 minutes and press Start/Pause.
9. Allow it to cool for 10 minutes before cutting.

Nutrition Value (Nutrition per Serving):

- Calories: 250
- Fat: 14.20g
- Carbohydrates: 35g
- Protein: 27.60g
- Sugar: 0g
- Cholesterol: 0g

Homemade Flamingos

Preparation time: 10 minutes. Cooking time: 20 minutes. Serve: 4

Ingredients:

- 400g of very thin sliced pork fillets c / n
- 2 boiled and chopped eggs
- 100g chopped Serrano ham
- 1 beaten egg
- Breadcrumbs

Direction:

1. Make a roll with the pork fillets. Introduce half cooked egg and Serrano ham. So that the roll does not lose its shape, fasten with a string or chopsticks.
2. Pass the rolls through beaten egg and then through the breadcrumbs until it forms a good layer.
3. Preheat the air fryer a few minutes at 180° C.
4. Insert the rolls in the basket and set the timer for about 8 minutes at 180o C.
5. Serve right away.

Nutrition Value (Nutrition per Serving):

- Calories: 424
- Fat: 15.15g
- Carbohydrates: 37.47g
- Protein: 31.84g
- Sugar: 3.37g
- Cholesterol: 157mg

North Carolina Style Pork Chops

Preparation time: 5 minutes. Cooking time: 10 minutes. Serve: 2

Ingredients:

- 2 boneless pork chops
- 15 ml of vegetable oil
- 25g dark brown sugar, packaged
- 6g of Hungarian paprika
- 2g ground mustard
- 2g freshly ground black pepper
- 3g onion powder
- 3g garlic powder
- Salt and pepper to taste

Direction:

1. Preheat the air fryer a few minutes at 180^0C.
2. Cover the pork chops with oil.
3. Put all the spices and season the pork chops abundantly, almost as if you were making them breaded.
4. Place the pork chops in the preheated air fryer.
5. Select Steak, set the time to 10 minutes.
6. Remove the pork chops when it has finished cooking. Let it stand for 5 minutes and serve.

Nutrition Value (Nutrition per Serving):

- Calories: 118
- Fat: 6.85g
- Carbohydrates: 0
- Protein: 13.12g
- Sugar: 0g
- Cholesterol: 39mg

Beef With Sesame And Ginger

Preparation time: 10 minutes. Cooking time: 23 minutes. Serve: 4-6

Ingredients:

- ½ cup tamari or soy sauce
- 3 tbsp olive oil
- 2 tbsp toasted sesame oil
- 1 tbsp brown sugar
- 1 tbsp ground fresh ginger
- 3 cloves garlic, minced
- 1 to 1½ pounds skirt steak, boneless sirloin, or low loin

Direction:

1. Put together the tamari sauce, oils, brown sugar, ginger, and garlic in small bowl. Add beef to a quarter-size plastic bag and pour the marinade into the bag. Press on the bag as much air as possible and seal it.

2. Refrigerate for 1 to 1½ hours, turning half the time. Remove the meat from the marinade and discard the marinade. Dry the meat with paper towels. Cook at a temperature of 350°F for 20 to 23 minutes, turning halfway through cooking.

Nutrition Value (Nutrition per Serving):

- Calories: 381
- Fat: 5g
- Carbohydrates: 9.6g
- Protein: 38g
- Sugar: 1.8g
- Cholesterol: 0mg

Katsu Pork

Preparation time: 10 minutes. Cooking time: 14 minutes. Serve: 2

Ingredients:

- 170g pork chops, boneless
- 56g of breadcrumbs
- 3g garlic powder
- 2g onion powder
- 6g of salt
- 1g white pepper
- 60g all-purpose flour
- 2 eggs, shakes
- Nonstick Spray Oil

Direction:

1. Place the pork chops in an airtight bag or cover them with a plastic wrap.
2. Crush the pork with a meat roller or hammer until it is 13 mm thick.
3. Combine the crumbs and seasonings in a bowl. Leave aside.
4. Pass each pork chop through the flour, then soak them in the beaten eggs and finally pass them through the crumb mixture.
5. Preheat the air fryer set the temperature to 180°C.
6. Spray pork chops on each side with cooking oil and place them in the preheated air fryer.
7. Cook the pork chops at 180°C for 4 minutes.
8. Remove them from the air fryer when finished and let them sit for 5 minutes.
9. Cut them into pieces and serve them.

Nutrition Value (Nutrition per Serving):

- Calories: 820
- Fat: 24.75g
- Carbohydrates: 117g
- Protein: 33.75g
- Sugar: 0g
- Cholesterol: 120mg

Pork on A Blanket

Preparation time: 5 minutes. Cooking time: 10 minutes. Serve: 4

Ingredients:

- ½ puff pastry sheet, defrosted
- 16 thick smoked sausages
- 15 ml of milk

Direction:

1. Preheat la air fryer to 200°C and set the timer to 5 minutes.
2. Cut the puff pastry into 64 x 38 mm strips.
3. Place a cocktail sausage at the end of the puff pastry and roll around the sausage, sealing the dough with some water.
4. Brush the top (with the seam facing down) of the sausages wrapped in milk and place them in the preheated air fryer.
5. Cook at 200°C for 10 minutes or until golden brown.

Nutrition Value (Nutrition per Serving):

- Calories: 242
- Fat: 14g
- Carbohydrates: 0g
- Protein: 27g
- Sugar: 0g
- Cholesterol: 80mg

Lamb Shawarma

Preparation time: 12 minutes. Cooking time: 8 minutes. Serve: 2

Ingredients:

- 340g ground lamb
- 2g cumin
- 2g of paprika
- 3g garlic powder
- 2g onion powder
- 1g of cinnamon
- 1g turmeric
- 1g fennel seeds
- 1g ground coriander seed
- 3g salt
- 4 bamboo skewers (229 mm)

Direction:

1. Put all the ingredients in a bowl and mix well.
2. Stir 85g of meat into each skewer, then place them in the fridge for 10 minutes.
3. Preheat in the air fryer to 200°C.
4. Place the skewers in the preheated air fryer, select Steak. Adjust to 8 minutes.
5. Serve with lemon yogurt dressing or alone.

Nutrition Value (Nutrition per Serving):

- Calories: 562
- Fat: 11.19g
- Carbohydrates: 76.89g
- Protein: 35.84g
- Sugar: 7.45g
- Cholesterol: 69mg

Stuffed Cabbage and Pork Loin Rolls

Preparation time: 5 minutes. Cooking time: 25 minutes. Serve: 4

Ingredients:

- 500g of white cabbage
- 1 onion
- 8 pork tenderloin steaks
- 2 carrots
- 4 tbsp soy sauce
- 50g of olive oil
- Salt
- 8 sheets of rice

Direction:

1. Put the chopped cabbage in the Thermomix glass together with the onion and the chopped carrot.
2. Select 5 seconds, speed 5. Add the extra virgin olive oil. Select 5 minutes, varoma temperature, left turn, spoon speed.
3. Cut the tenderloin steaks into thin strips. Add the meat to the Thermomix glass. Select 5 minutes, varoma temperature, left turn, spoon speed. Without beaker
4. Add the soy sauce. Select 5 minutes, varoma temperature, left turn, spoon speed. Rectify salt. Let it cold down.
5. Hydrate the rice slices. Extend and distribute the filling between them.
6. Make the rolls, folding so that the edges are completely closed. Place the rolls in the air fryer and paint with the oil.
7. Select 10 minutes, 180^0C.

Nutrition Value (Nutrition per Serving):

- Calories: 120
- Fat: 3.41g
- Carbohydrates: 0g
- Protein: 20.99g
- Sugar: 0g
- Cholesterol: 65mg

Pork Head Chops with Vegetables

Preparation time: 5 minutes. Cooking time: 20 minutes. Serve: 2-4

Ingredients:

- 4 pork head chops
- 2 red tomatoes
- 1 large green pepper
- 4 mushrooms
- 1 onion
- 4 slices of cheese
- Salt
- Ground pepper
- Extra virgin olive oil

Direction:

1. Put the four chops on a plate and salt and pepper.
2. Put two of the chops in the air fryer basket.
3. Place tomato slices, cheese slices, pepper slices, onion slices and mushroom slices. Add some threads of oil.
4. Take the air fryer and select 180^0C, 15 minutes.
5. Check that the meat is well made and take out.
6. Repeat the same operation with the other two pork chops.

Nutrition Value (Nutrition per Serving):

- Calories: 106
- Fat: 5g
- Carbohydrates: 2g
- Protein: 11g
- Sugar: 0g
- Cholesterol: 0mg

Provencal Ribs

Preparation time: 10 minutes. Cooking time: 1h 20 minutes. Serve: 4

Ingredients:

- 500g of pork ribs
- Provencal herbs
- Salt
- Ground pepper
- Oil

Direction:

1. Put the ribs in a bowl and add some oil, Provencal herbs, salt, and ground pepper.
2. Stir well and leave in the fridge for at least 1 hour.
3. Put the ribs in the basket of the air fryer and select 200^0C, 20 minutes.
4. From time to time shake the basket and remove the ribs.

Nutrition Value (Nutrition per Serving):

- Calories: 296
- Fat: 22.63g
- Carbohydrates: 0g
- Protein: 21.71g
- Sugar: 0g
- Cholesterol: 90mg

Beef Scallops

Preparation time: 15 minutes. Cooking time: 20 minutes. Serve: 4

Ingredients:

- 16 veal scallops
- Salt
- Ground pepper
- Garlic powder
- 2 eggs
- Breadcrumbs
- Extra virgin olive oil

Direction:

1. Put the beef scallops well spread and salt and pepper. Add some garlic powder.
2. In a bowl, beat the eggs.
3. In another bowl put the breadcrumbs.
4. Pass the Beef scallops for beaten egg and then for the breadcrumbs.
5. Spray with extra virgin olive oil on both sides.
6. Put a batch in the basket of the air fryer. Do not pile the scallops too much.
7. Select 180^0C, 15 minutes. From time to time shake the basket so that the scallops move.
8. When finishing that batch, put the next one and so on until you finish with everyone, usually 4 or 5 scallops enter per batch.

Nutrition Value (Nutrition per Serving):

- Calories: 330
- Fat: 16.27g
- Carbohydrates: 0g
- Protein: 43g
- Sugar: 0g
- Cholesterol: 163mg

Potatoes with Loin and Cheese

Preparation time: 10 minutes. Cooking time: 30 minutes. Serve: 4

Ingredients:

- 1kg of potatoes
- 1 large onion
- 1 piece of roasted loin
- Extra virgin olive oil
- Salt
- Ground pepper
- Grated cheese

Direction:

1. Peel the potatoes, cut the cane, wash, and dry.
2. Put salt and add some threads of oil, we bind well.
3. Pass the potatoes to the basket of the air fryer and select 180^0C, 20 minutes.
4. Meanwhile, in a pan, put some extra virgin olive oil and add the peeled onion and cut into julienne.
5. When the onion is transparent, add the chopped loin.
6. Sauté well and pepper.
7. Put the potatoes on a baking sheet.
8. Add the onion with the loin.
9. Cover with a layer of grated cheese.
10. Bake a little until the cheese takes heat and melts.

Nutrition Value (Nutrition per Serving):

- Calories: 332
- Fat: 7g
- Carbohydrates: 41g
- Protein: 23g
- Sugar: 0g
- Cholesterol: 0mg

Potatoes with Loin and Cheese

Preparation time: 10 minutes. Cooking time: 30 minutes. Serve: 4

Ingredients:

- 1kg of potatoes
- 1 large onion
- 1 piece of roasted loin
- Extra virgin olive oil
- Salt
- Ground pepper
- Grated cheese

Direction:

1. Peel the potatoes, cut the cane, wash, and dry.
2. Put salt and add some threads of oil, bind well.
3. Pass the potatoes to the basket of the air fryer and select 180^0C, 20 minutes.
4. Meanwhile, in a pan, put some extra virgin olive oil and add the peeled onion and cut into julienne.
5. When the onion is transparent, add the chopped loin.
6. Sauté well and pepper.
7. Put the potatoes on a baking sheet.
8. Add the onion with the loin.
9. Cover with a layer of grated cheese.
10. Bake a little until the cheese takes heat and melts.

Nutrition Value (Nutrition per Serving):

- Calories: 332
- Fat: 7g
- Carbohydrates: 41g
- Protein: 23g
- Sugar: 0g
- Cholesterol: 0mg

Russian Steaks with Nuts and Cheese

Preparation time: 5 minutes. Cooking time: 20 minutes. Serve: 4

Ingredients:

- 800g of minced pork
- 200g of cream cheese
- 50g peeled walnuts
- 1 onion
- Salt
- Ground pepper
- 1 egg
- Breadcrumbs
- Extra virgin olive oil

Direction:

1. Put the onion cut into quarters in the Thermomix glass and select 5 seconds speed 5.
2. Add the minced meat, cheese, egg, salt, and pepper.
3. Select 10 seconds, speed 5, turn left.
4. Add the chopped and peeled walnuts and select 4 seconds, turn left, speed 5.
5. Pass the dough to a bowl.
6. Make Russian steaks and go through breadcrumbs.
7. Paint the Russian fillets with extra virgin olive oil on both sides with a brush.
8. Put in the basket of the air fryer, without stacking the Russian fillets.
9. Select 180^0C, 15 minutes.

Nutrition Value (Nutrition per Serving):

- Calories: 36
- Fat: 20g
- Carbohydrates: 6g
- Protein: 46g
- Sugar: 0g
- Cholesterol: 63mg

Potatoes with Bacon, Onion and Cheese

Preparation time: 10 minutes. Cooking time: 15 minutes. Serve: 4

Ingredients:

- 200g potatoes
- 150g bacon
- 1 onion
- Slices of cheese
- Extra virgin olive oil
- Salt

Direction:

1. Peel the potatoes, cut into thin slices, and wash them well.
2. Drain and dry the potatoes, put salt and a few strands of extra virgin olive oil.
3. Stir well and place in the basket of the air fryer.
4. Cut the onion into julienne, put a little oil, and stir, place on the potatoes.
5. Finally, put the sliced bacon on the onion.
6. Take the basket to the air fryer and select 20 minutes, 180^0C.
7. From time to time, remove the basket.
8. Take all the contents of the basket to a source and when it is still hot, place the slices of cheese on top.
9. You can let the heat of the potatoes melt the cheese or you can gratin a few minutes in the oven.

Nutrition Value (Nutrition per Serving):

- Calories: 125
- Fat: 2g
- Carbohydrates: 24g
- Protein: 5g
- Sugar: 0.1g
- Cholesterol: 40mg

Pork Liver

Preparation time: 5 minutes. Cooking time: 15 minutes. Serve: 4

Ingredients:

- 500g of pork liver cut into steaks
- Breadcrumbs
- Salt
- Ground pepper
- 1 lemon
- Extra virgin olive oil

Direction:

1. Put the steaks on a plate or bowl.
2. Add the lemon juice, salt, and ground pepper.
3. Leave a few minutes to macerate the pork liver fillets.
4. Drain well and go through breadcrumbs, it is not necessary to pass the fillets through beaten egg because the liver is very moist, the breadcrumbs are perfectly glued.
5. Spray with extra virgin olive oil. If you don't have a sprayer, paint with a silicone brush.
6. Put the pork liver fillets in the air fryer basket.
7. Program 180^0C, 10 minutes.
8. Take out if you see them golden to your liking and put another batch.
9. You should not pile the pork liver fillets, which are well extended so that the empanada is crispy on all sides.

Nutrition Value (Nutrition per Serving):

- Calories: 134
- Fat: 3.65g
- Carbohydrates: 2.47g
- Protein: 21.39g

Marinated Loin Potatoes

Preparation time: 10 minutes. Cooking time: 1h. Serve: 2

Ingredients:

- 2 medium potatoes
- 4 fillets of marinated loin
- A little extra virgin olive oil
- Salt

Direction:

1. Peel the potatoes and cut. Cut with match-sized mandolin, potatoes with a cane but very thin.
2. Wash and immerse in water 30 minutes.
3. Drain and dry well.
4. Add a little oil and stir so that the oil permeates well in all the potatoes.
5. Go to the basket of the air fryer and distribute well.
6. Select 160°C, 10 minutes.
7. Take out the basket, shake so that the potatoes take off. Let the potato tender. If it is not, leave 5 more minutes.
8. Place the steaks on top of the potatoes.
9. Select 160°C, 10 minutes and 180 degrees 5 minutes again.

Nutrition Value (Nutrition per Serving):

- Calories: 136
- Fat: 5.1g
- Carbohydrates: 1.9g
- Protein: 20.7g
- Sugar: 0.4g
- Cholesterol: 65mg

Pork Fritters

Preparation time: 5 minutes. Cooking time: 20 minutes. Serve: 2-4

Ingredients:

- Pork fillets cut into pieces
- 264g flour
- ½ tsp salt
- ½ tsp ground paprika
- A pinch of cayenne pepper
- 500 ml of sparkling water
- Flour to cover
- Nonstick cooking spray

Direction:

1. Coat the pork pieces with flour, shaking off the excess.
2. Mix the flour, seasonings and carbonated water creating a dough in a medium container. Beat until smooth.
3. Preheat the air fryer to 360°F (182°C).
4. Introduce previously sprinkled pork into the dough.
5. Spray the basket of the air fryer with nonstick cooking spray
6. Place the battered pork pieces in the air fryer basket in a single layer.
7. Cook the pork for 10 to 12 minutes, turning it in the middle of the process.
8. Pork fritters will be ready when the breaded has a brown-gold color and the pork is fully cooked.

Nutrition Value (Nutrition per Serving):

- Calories: 412
- Fat: 18.30g
- Carbohydrates: 59.5g
- Protein: 3.10g
- Sugar: 35.11g
- Cholesterol: 11mg

Pork Tenderloin

Preparation time: 10 minutes. Cooking time: 45 minutes. Serve: 2-4

Ingredients:

- 2 large eggs
- ¼ cup milk
- 2 cups seasoned breadcrumbs
- Salt and pepper to taste
- Nonstick cooking spray

Direction:

1. Slice the tenderloin into ½ inch slices.
2. Place the slices between two plastic sheets and tap them until each piece is ¼ inch thick.
3. In a large container, mix the eggs and milk.
4. In a separate container or dish, pour the breadcrumbs.
5. Introduce each piece of pork in the mixture of eggs and milk, letting the excess drain.
6. Then introduce the pork in the breadcrumbs, covering each side.
7. Place the covered pork on a wire rack for 30 minutes to make sure the cover adheres.
8. Preheat the air fryer to 400°F (204 °C).
9. Spray the basket of the air fryer with nonstick cooking spray. Place the covered sirloin in the basket in a single layer.
10. Cook the sirloin for 10 minutes, then take it out, turn it over and sprinkle with more nonstick spray.
11. Cook for 5-minutes more or until both sides are crispy and golden brown.

Nutrition Value (Nutrition per Serving):

- Calories: 158
- Fat: 7.12g
- Carbohydrates: 0g
- Protein: 22.05g
- Sugar: 0g
- Cholesterol: 67mg

Cheesy Beef Paseíllo

Preparation time: 10 minutes. Cooking time: 20 minutes. Serve: 15

Ingredients:

- 1-2 tbsp olive oil
- 2 pounds lean ground beef
- ½ chopped onion
- 2 cloves garlic, minced
- ½ tbsp Adobo seasoning
- 2 tsp dried oregano
- 1 packet of optional seasoning
- 2 tbsp chopped cilantro
- ¼ cup grated cheese
- 15 dough disks
- 15 slices of yellow cheese

Direction:

1. In a large skillet over medium-high heat, heat the oil. Once the oil has warmed, add the meat, onions, and Adobo seasoning.
2. Brown veal, about 6-7 minutes. Drain the ground beef. Add the remaining seasonings and cilantro. Cook an additional minute. Add grated cheese, if desired. Melt the cheese.
3. On each dough disk, add a slice of cheese to the center and add 3-4 tablespoons of meat mixture over the slice of cheese. Fold over the dough disk, and with a fork, fold the edges and set it aside.
4. Preheat the air fryer to 370^0C for 3 minutes.
5. Once three minutes have passed, spray the air fryer pan with cooking spray and add 3-4 cupcakes to the basket. Close the basket and set to 370^0C and cook for 7 minutes. After 7 minutes, verify it. Cook up to 3 additional minutes, or the desired level of sharpness, if desired.
6. Repeat until finished.

Nutrition Value (Nutrition per Serving):

- Calories: 225
- Fat: 5g
- Carbohydrates: 10g
- Protein: 10g
- Sugar: 0g
- Cholesterol: 25mg

Beef Patty

Preparation time: 20 minutes. Cooking time: 30 minutes. Serve: 4

Ingredients:

- Prepared dough
- 300g beef
- 1 large onion
- 1 red pepper
- 2 hard-boiled eggs
- Salt
- Pepper to taste.
- 1 tsp oil

Direction:

1. Remove the dough from the refrigerator 10 minutes before.
2. In a pan, place oil, 1 onion, 1 pepper, garlic, seasoning. Add ground beef until cooked well. Season with salt and pepper to taste.
3. Let the filling cool
4. Place the filling in each circle of the dough and seal with egg white at the edges.
5. Butter a refractory mold and accommodate the patty.
6. Preheat the oven to 190°C for 10 minutes by pressing the Convection button
7. Place the refractory on the metal rack and bring to the preheated oven for 30 minutes at 190°C.

Nutrition Value (Nutrition per Serving):

- Calories: 263
- Fat: 17.25g
- Carbohydrates: 20.22g
- Protein: 6.65g
- Sugar: 0.96g
- Cholesterol: 59mg

Roasted Pork

Preparation time: 5 minutes. Cooking time: 30 minutes. Serve: 2-4

Ingredients:

- 500-2000g Pork meat (To roast)
- Salt
- Oil

Direction:

1. Join the cuts in an orderly manner.
2. Place the meat on the plate
3. Varnish with a little oil.
4. Place the roasts with the fat side down.
5. Cook in air fryer at 180^0C for 30 minutes.
6. Turn when you hear the beep.
7. Remove from the oven. Drain excess juice.
8. Let stand for 10 minutes on aluminum foil before serving.

Nutrition Value (Nutrition per Serving):

- Calories: 820
- Fat: 24.75g
- Carbohydrates: 117g
- Protein: 33.75g
- Sugar: 0g
- Cholesterol: 120mg

Fried Pork Chops

Preparation time: 5 minutes. Cooking time: 35 minutes. Serve: 2

Ingredients:

- 3 cloves of ground garlic
- 2 tbsp olive oil
- 1 tbsp of marinade
- 4 thawed pork chops

Direction:

1. Mix the cloves of ground garlic, marinade, and oil. Then apply this mixture on the chops.
2. Put the chops in the air fryer at 360^0C for 35 minutes.

Nutrition Value (Nutrition per Serving):

- Calories: 118
- Fat: 6.85g
- Carbohydrates: 0
- Protein: 13.12g
- Sugar: 0g
- Cholesterol: 39mg

Crispy Pork Chops

Preparation time: 5 minutes. Cooking time: 12 minutes. Serve: 4

Ingredients:

- Olive oil spray
- 6 (3/4-inch thick) central cut boneless pork chops, trimmed fat (5 oz each)
- Kosher salt
- 1 large egg, beaten
- ½ cup panko crumbs (check labels for GF)
- 1/3 cup crushed corn crumbs
- 2 tbsp grated Parmesan cheese (skip for vegetarians)
- 1 ¼ tsp sweet paprika
- ½ tsp garlic powder
- ½ tsp onion powder
- ¼ tsp chili powder
- 1/8 tsp black pepper

Direction:

1. Preheat the fryer with air at 400^0F for 12 minutes and lightly spray the basket with oil.
2. Season the pork chops on both sides with ½ teaspoon of kosher salt.
3. Put the panko, corn crumbs, Parmesan cheese, ¾ teaspoon kosher salt, paprika, garlic powder, onion powder, chili powder and black pepper in a large, shallow bowl.
4. Place the beaten egg in another. Dip the pork in the egg, then the crumb mixture.
5. When the fryer is ready, place 3 of the chops in the prepared basket and sprinkle the top with oil.
6. Cook 12 minutes turning in half, sprinkling both sides with oil. Set aside and repeat with the rest.

Nutrition Value (Nutrition per Serving):

- Calories: 378
- Fat: 13g
- Carbohydrates: 8g
- Protein: 33g
- Sugar: 1 g
- Cholesterol: 121 mg

Pork Bondiola Chop

Preparation time: 5 minutes. Cooking time: 20 minutes. Serve: 4

Ingredients:

- 1kg bondiola in pieces
- Breadcrumbs
- 2 eggs
- Seasoning to taste

Direction:

1. Cut the bondiola into small pieces, seasonings to taste.
2. Beat the eggs.
3. Pass the bondiola seasoned by beaten egg and then by breadcrumbs.
4. Then place in the air fryer for 20 minutes, halfway around turn and ready snacks of bondiola.

Nutrition Value (Nutrition per Serving):

- Calories: 265
- Fat: 20.36g
- Carbohydrates: 0g
- Protein: 19.14g
- Sugar: 0g
- Cholesterol: 146mg

Pork Taquitos

Preparation time: 10 minutes. Cooking time: 15 minutes. Serve: 6

Ingredients:

- 3 cups shredded pork loin (previously cooked)
- Lemon juice
- 10 templates
- 2 cups mozzarella cheese
- Cooking spray (oil)
- Sauce to taste
- Sour cream to taste

Direction:

1. Preheat the fryer to 380 degrees F. Meanwhile, soften the templates in the microwave for 10 seconds.
2. On the other hand, in a bowl add the pork with a pinch of lemon.
3. Then, add the shredded pork and cheese to the template. Roll up the template and close.
4. Once ready, add spray on them and take to the air fryer for 10 minutes.

Nutrition Value (Nutrition per Serving):

- Calories: 133
- Fat: 4g
- Carbohydrates: 22g
- Protein: 5g
- Sugar: 0g
- Cholesterol: 0mg

Pork Knuckle

Preparation time: 15 minutes. Cooking time: 50 minutes. Serve: 2

Ingredients:

Knuckle:

- 3 potatoes
- 1 head of garlic
- Water
- Extra virgin olive oil
- Salt
- Peppercorns
- 1 bay leaf
- Vinaigrette
- Mustard and beer (to accompany)

For the sauerkraut:

- 1 cabbage
- 100g of butter
- 1 glass of white wine
- 5 tbsp vinegar
- a pinch of cumin
- Some coriander seeds
- Peppercorns
- Juniper berries

Direction:

1. Cook the knuckle in a quick pot with the potatoes and a little salt. Add some pepper balls, a bay leaf, and a garlic head. Cover with water and cook for 40 minutes. When it starts to boil, lower the heat to medium heat.

2. For sauerkraut, chop the cabbage into quarters and cut into strips with the mandolin. Put the cabbage in a bowl, water with a glass of white wine and a dash of vinegar and mix everything well.

3. Crush some juniper berries with a knife, add them and sprinkle with pepper, coriander, and cumin. Mix the whole well, wet with a glass of water and let stand for 3 days or more. Cook the cabbage for 15 minutes in a pot, drain and sauté over medium heat for 8 minutes. Season and water with a dash of olive oil.

4. Pass the knuckle in the air fryer basket, dip extra virgin olive oil at 250°C for 10 minutes. Serve the knuckle with potatoes and sauerkraut.

Nutrition Value (Nutrition per Serving):

- Calories: 333
- Fat: 22g
- Carbohydrates: 0g
- Protein: 28g
- Sugar: 0g
- Cholesterol: 84mg

Chapter 6: Seafood and Fish recipes

Cajun Style Shrimp

Preparation time: 3 minutes. Cooking time: 10 minutes. Serve: 2

Ingredients:

- 6g of salt
- 2g smoked paprika
- 2g garlic powder
- 2g Italian seasoning
- 2g chili powder
- 1g onion powder
- 1g cayenne pepper
- 1g black pepper
- 1g dried thyme
- 454g large shrimp, peeled and unveiled
- 30 ml of olive oil
- Lime wedges, to serve

Direction:

1. Select Preheat, in the air fryer, set the temperature to 190°C and press Start/Pause.
2. Combine all seasonings in a large bowl. Set aside
3. Mix the shrimp with olive oil until they are evenly coated.
4. Sprinkle the dressing mixture over the shrimp and stir until well coated.
5. Place the shrimp in the preheated air fryer.
6. Select Shrimp set the time to 5 minutes and press Start/Pause.
7. Shake the baskets in the middle of cooking.
8. Serve with pieces of lime.

Nutrition Value (Nutrition per Serving):

- Calories: 126
- Fat: 6g
- Carbohydrates: 2g
- Proteins: 33g
- Cholesterol: 199mg
- Sodium: 231mg

Crab Cakes

Preparation time: 10 minutes. Cooking time: 40 minutes. Serve: 2

Ingredients:

For crab cakes:

- 1 large egg, beaten
- 17g of mayonnaise
- 11g Dijon mustard
- 5 ml Worcestershire sauce
- 2g Old Bay seasoning
- 2g of salt
- A pinch of white pepper
- A pinch of cayenne
- 26g celery, finely diced
- 45g red pepper, finely diced
- 8g fresh parsley, finely chopped
- 227g of crab meat
- 28g breadcrumbs
- Nonstick Spray Oil

Remodeled:

- 55g of mayonnaise
- 15g capers, washed and drained
- 5g sweet pickles, chopped
- 5g red onion, finely chopped
- 8 ml of lemon juice
- 8g Dijon mustard
- Salt and pepper to taste

Direction:

1. Mix the ingredients of remodeled until everything is well incorporated. Set aside
2. Beat the egg, mayonnaise, mustard, Worcestershire sauce, Old Bay seasoning, salt, white pepper, cayenne pepper, celery, pepper, and parsley.
3. Gently stir the crab meat in the egg mixture and stir it until well mixed.
4. Sprinkle the breadcrumbs over the crab mixture and fold them gently until the breadcrumbs cover every corner.
5. Shape the crab mixture into 4 cakes and chill in the fridge for 30 minutes.
6. Select Preheat in the air fryer and press Start/Pause.
7. Place a sheet of baking paper in the basket of the preheated air fryer. Sprinkle the crab cakes with cooking spray and place them gently on the paper.

8. Cook the crab cakes at 205°C for 8 minutes until golden brown.

9. Flip crab cakes during cooking.

10. Serve with remodeled.

Nutrition Value (Nutrition per Serving):

- Calories: 110
- Fat: 6.5g
- Carbohydrates: 5.5g
- Protein: 7g
- Sugar: 2g

Tuna Pie

Preparation time: 10 minutes. Cooking time: 30 minutes. Serving: 4

Ingredients:

- 2 hard-boiled eggs
- 2 tuna cans
- 200 ml fried tomato
- 1 sheet of broken dough.

Direction:

1. Cut the eggs into small pieces and mix with the tuna and tomato.
2. Spread the sheet of broken dough and cut into two equal squares.
3. Put the mixture of tuna, eggs, and tomato on one of the squares.
4. Cover with the other, join at the ends and decorate with leftover little pieces.
5. Preheat the air fryer a few minutes at 180^0C.
6. Enter in the air fryer basket and set the timer for 15 minutes at 180^0C

Nutrition Value (Nutrition per Serving):

- Calories: 244
- Fat: 13.67g
- Carbohydrates: 21.06g
- Protein: 8.72g
- Sugar: 0.22g
- Cholesterol: 59mg

Tuna Puff Pastry

Preparation time: 5 minutes. Cooking time: 15 minutes. Serving: 2

Ingredients:

- 2 square puff pastry dough, bought ready
- 1 egg (white and yolk separated)
- ½ cup tuna tea
- ½ cup chopped parsley tea
- ½ cup chopped tea olives
- Salt and pepper to taste

Direction:

1. Preheat the air fryer. Set the timer of 5 minutes and the temperature to 200C.

2. Mix the tuna with olives and parsley. Season to taste and set aside. Place half of the filling in each dough and fold in half. Brush with egg white and close gently. After closing, make two small cuts at the top of the air outlet. Brush with the egg yolk.

3. Place in the basket of the air fryer. Set the time to 10 minutes and press the power button.

Nutrition Value (Nutrition per Serving):

- Calories: 291
- Fat: 16g
- Carbohydrates: 26g
- Protein: 8g
- Sugar: 0g
- Cholesterol: 0

Cajun Style Catfish

Preparation time: 3 minutes. Cooking time: 7 minutes. Serve: 2

Ingredients:

- 5g of paprika
- 3g garlic powder
- 2g onion powder
- 2g ground dried thyme
- 1g ground black pepper
- 1g cayenne pepper
- 1g dried basil
- 1g dried oregano
- 2 catfish fillets (6 oz)
- Nonstick Spray Oil

Direction:

1. Preheat the air fryer for a few minutes. Set the temperature to 175°C.
2. Mix all seasonings in a bowl.
3. Cover the fish generously on each side with the dressing mixture.
4. Spray each side of the fish with oil spray and place it in the preheated air fryer.
5. Select Marine Food and press Start /Pause.
6. Remove carefully when you finish cooking and serve on semolina.

Nutrition Value (Nutrition per Serving):

- Calories: 228
- Fat; 13g
- Carbohydrates: 0g
- Protein: 20g
- Sugar: 0g
- Cholesterol: 71mg

Tuna Chipotle

Preparation time: 5 minutes. Cooking time: 8 minutes. Serve: 2

Ingredients:

- 142g tuna
- 45g chipotle sauce
- 4 slices of white bread
- 2 slices of pepper jack cheese

Direction:

1. Preheat the air fryer set the temperature to 160°C.
2. Mix the tuna and chipotle until combined.
3. Spread half of the chipotle tuna mixture on each of the 2 slices of bread.
4. Add a slice of pepper jack cheese on each and close with the remaining 2 slices of bread, making 2 sandwiches.
5. Place the sandwiches in the preheated air fryer. Set the timer to 8 minutes.
6. Cut diagonally and serve.

Nutrition Value (Nutrition per Serving):

- Calories: 121
- Fat: 4g
- Carbohydrates: 2g
- Protein: 16g
- Sugar: 0g
- Cholesterol: 36mg

Fish Tacos

Preparation time: 10 minutes. Cooking time: 7 minutes. Serve: 4-5

Ingredients:

- 454g of tilapia, cut into strips of 38 mm thick
- 52g yellow cornmeal
- 1g ground cumin
- 1g chili powder
- 2g garlic powder
- 1g onion powder
- 3g of salt
- 1g black pepper
- Nonstick Spray Oil
- Corn tortillas, to serve
- Tartar sauce, to serve
- Lime wedges, to serve

Direction:

1. Cut the tilapia into strips 38 mm thick.
2. Mix cornmeal and seasonings in a shallow dish.
3. Cover the fish strips with seasoned cornmeal. Set aside in the fridge.
4. Preheat the air fryer for 5 minutes. Set the temperature to 170°C.
5. Sprinkle the fish coated with oil spray and place it in the preheated air fryer.
6. Put the fish in the air fryer, set the timer to 7 minutes.
7. Turn the fish halfway through cooking.
8. Serve the fish in corn tortillas with tartar sauce and a splash of lemon.

Nutrition Value (Nutrition per Serving):

- Calories: 108
- Fat: 26g
- Carbohydrates: 11g
- Protein: 9g
- Sugar: 0g
- Cholesterol: 56mg

Teriyaki Glazed Salmon

Preparation time: 10 minutes. Cooking time: 8 minutes. Serve: 2

Ingredients:

- Teriyaki sauce:
- 118 ml soy sauce
- 50g of sugar
- 1g grated ginger
- 1 clove garlic, crushed
- 60 ml of orange juice

Salmon:

- 2 salmon fillets (5 oz)
- 20 ml of vegetable oil
- Salt and white pepper, to taste

Direction:

1. Put all the ingredients of the teriyaki sauce in a small pot.
2. Boil the sauce, reduce by half, then let it cool.
3. Preheat the air fryer set the temperature to 180°C.
4. Cover the salmon with oil and season with salt and white pepper.
5. Place the salmon in the preheated air and adjust to 8 minutes.
6. Remove the salmon from the fryer when finished. Let stand for 5 minutes, then glaze with teriyaki sauce.
7. Serve on a bed of white rice or grilled vegetables.

Nutrition Value (Nutrition per Serving):

- Calories: 223
- Fat: 6g
- Carbohydrates: 15g
- Protein: 10g
- Sugar: 15g
- Cholesterol: 0mg

Salmon With Butter And Lemon

Preparation time: 3 minutes. Cooking time: 8 minutes. Serve: 2

Ingredients:

- 2 salmon fillets
- Salt and pepper to taste
- Nonstick Spray Oil
- 30g butter
- 30 ml of fresh lemon juice
- 1 clove garlic, grated
- 6 ml Worcestershire sauce

Direction:

1. Season the salmon to taste with salt and pepper.
2. Preheat the air fryer set the temperature to 175°C for 5 minutes.
3. Spray the baskets of the preheated air fryer with oil spray and place the fish inside.
4. Put the salmon in the air fryer for 8 minutes.
5. Mix the butter, lemon juice, garlic and Worcestershire sauce in a small saucepan and melt over low heat, about 1 minute.
6. Serve the salmon fillets with rice and cover with the lemon butter sauce.

Nutrition Value (Nutrition per Serving):

- Calories: 412
- Lipids: 24.7g
- Carbohydrates: 0.0g
- Proteins: 44.2g
- Sugars: 0.0g
- Cholesterol: 126mg

Crispy Fish Nuggets

Preparation time: 6 minutes. Cooking time: 6 minutes. Serve: 2

Ingredients:

- 454g of white fish or other soft fish, cut into strips 38 x 13 mm long
- 30g all-purpose flour
- 7g Old Bay seasoning
- 2 eggs, shakes
- 180g breadcrumbs
- Nonstick Spray Oil
- Tartar sauce, to serve

Direction:

1. Cut the fish into strips 38 x 13 mm long.
2. Mix the flour and the Old Bay seasoning in a bowl.
3. Cover each piece of fish with seasoned flour and then dip in the beaten eggs and stir in breadcrumbs.
4. Preheat the air fryer set the temperature and time to 175°C and 5 minutes.
5. Spray the fish on both sides with spray oil and place it in the preheated air fryer.
6. Select Frozen Meals, set the time to 6 minutes and press Start/Pause.
7. Shake the baskets in the middle of cooking.

Nutrition Value (Nutrition per Serving):

- Calories: 196
- Fat: 11g
- Carbohydrates: 1g
- Protein: 13g
- Sugar: 1g
- Cholesterol: 31mg

Bacon Wrapped Shrimp

Preparation time: 5 minutes. Cooking time: 16 minutes. Serve: 4-5

Ingredients:

- 16 giant shrimp, peeled and vein free
- 3g garlic powder
- 2g of paprika
- 2g onion powder
- 1g ground black pepper
- 8 bacon strips, cut lengthwise

Direction:

1. Place the giant shrimp in a bowl and season with spices.
2. Wrap the bacon around the shrimp, starting from the head to the tail and secure with sticks.
3. Select Preheat, set the temperature to 160°C.
4. Add half of the shrimp to the preheated air fryer.
5. Select Bacon and press Start / Pause. When cooking is finished, set them aside.
6. Repeat with the next batch of shrimp
7. Remove excess fat with a paper towel and serve.

Nutrition Value (Nutrition per Serving):

- Calories: 283
- Fat: 19g
- Carbohydrates: 14g
- Protein: 14g
- Sugar: 12g
- Cholesterol: 105mg

Coconut Shrimp

Preparation time: 8 minutes. Cooking time: 8 minutes. Serve: 3

Ingredients:

- 1 ½ lb. shrimp
- ¾ cup flour
- 1 egg
- 2 cups shredded coconut
- 1 cup of milk
- ½ cup onion

Direction:

1. Mix the flour and half of the dressings in a bowl. Beat the eggs together with the milk in a separate bowl.
2. Put the breadcrumbs, coconut and the other half of the dressings and spices in an additional bowl.
3. Cover each shrimp with flour, then dip it in egg and pass it through the bread and coconut. Dip it again in egg and bread. Set aside.
4. Preheat the air fryer for a few minutes. Set the temperature to 175°C.
5. Add shrimp evenly to the air fryer. Set the time to 8 minutes and sprinkle with nonstick spray oil.
6. Be sure to turn the shrimp halfway through cooking

Nutrition Value (Nutrition per Serving):

- Energy: 949
- Fat: 44.61g
- Carbohydrates: 119g
- Protein: 30.47g
- Sugar: 26g
- Cholesterol: 176mg

Easy Salmon

Preparation time: 5 minutes. Cooking time: 20 minutes. Serve: 2

Ingredients:

- 2 thick salmon fillets
- ½ lemon juice
- 1 clove garlic
- Salt and pepper to taste
- Olive oil for brushing

Direction:

1. Preheat the air fryer. Set the time of 5 minutes and the temperature to 200^0C.
2. Wash the salmon slices with lemon juice and season with garlic, salt, and pepper to taste.
3. Place the salmon with the skin facing down in the basket of the air fryer.
4. Brush with olive oil. Set the time of 15 minutes and press the power button. Turn salmon slices in half the time to leave cooked equally.

Nutrition Value (Nutrition per Serving):

- Energy: 191
- Fat: 12.10g
- Carbohydrates: 0g
- Protein: 20.62g
- Sugar: 0g
- Cholesterol: 48.10mg

Hake With Roasted Peppers

Preparation time: 5 minutes. Cooking time: 15 minutes. Serve: 2

Ingredients:

- 4 large hake fillets
- Egg and breadcrumbs
- Salt
- Ground pepper
- Extra virgin olive oil
- Roasted and seasoned peppers

Direction:

1. Roast the peppers in advance and once they are cold, peel and cut.
2. Chop onion and season with salt, extra virgin olive oil and vinegar.
3. Season the hake fillets.
4. Go through beaten egg and then breadcrumbs.
5. Paint well with extra virgin olive oil.
6. Place in the basket of the air fryer and select 15 minutes 180^0C.
7. Serve the hake with the roasted peppers.

Nutrition Value (Nutrition per Serving):

- Calories: 132
- Fat: 4.38g
- Carbohydrates: 0.41g
- Protein: 21.38g
- Sugar: 0.09g
- Cholesterol: 178mg

Mushrooms Stuffed With Tuna

Preparation time: 5 minutes. Cooking time: 10 minutes. Serve: 4

Ingredients:

- 8 large mushrooms
- 1 can of tuna
- Mayonnaise

Direction:

1. Remove the trunks to the mushrooms and reserve for another recipe.
2. Peel the mushrooms and place in the basket of the air fryer, face down.
3. Select 160^0C, 10 minutes.
4. Take out and let cool.
5. In a bowl, mix the well-drained tuna with a little mayonnaise, just to make the tuna juicy and compact.
6. Fill the mushrooms with the tuna and mayonnaise mixture.

Nutrition Value (Nutrition per Serving):

- Calories: 150
- Fat: 6g
- Carbohydrates: 1g
- Protein: 8g
- Sugar: 0g
- Cholesterol: 15mg

Hake Fillets With Salad

Preparation time: 5 minutes. Cooking time: 20 minutes. Serve: 4

Ingredients:

- 8 hake fillets
- Flour, egg, and breadcrumbs for breading
- 1 lettuce
- 1 bag of canons
- Slices of cooked ham
- Extra virgin olive oil
- Sherry vinegar
- Salt

Direction:

1. Season the hake fillets.
2. Breaded, passed through flour, beaten egg and breadcrumbs.
3. Place in the air fryer and paint with oil.
4. Select 180^0C, 20 minutes. Make hake fillets in batches.
5. Prepare the salad, in a bowl put the lettuce chopped with the canons and add salt, vinegar and oil.
6. Bind and add the chopped cooked ham.
7. Serve the hake fillets with the salad.

Nutrition Value (Nutrition per Serving):

- Calories: 132
- Fat: 4.38g
- Carbohydrates: 0.41g
- Protein: 21.38g
- Sugar: 0.09g
- Cholesterol: 178mg

Hake Breaded With Red Peppers Cream

Preparation time: 5 minutes. Cooking time: 20 minutes. Serve: 4

Ingredients:

- 4 frozen breaded hake fillets
- 1 large onion
- 1 large or 2 medium red pepper
- 200 ml of cooking cream
- Extra virgin olive oil
- Salt
- Ground pepper

Direction:

1. Cut the onion and pepper in julienne and put it in a pan with a little extra virgin olive oil over medium-low heat to sauté.
2. Place the hake fillets in the basket of the air fryer and paint with a silicone brush and oil.
3. Select 180^0C about 20 minutes or so.
4. While the hake fillets are made, return to the peppers. When they are tender, add the cream, salt, and pepper.
5. Boil so that the cream reduces.

Nutrition Value (Nutrition per Serving):

- Calories: 132
- Fat: 4.38g
- Carbohydrates: 0.41g
- Protein: 21.38g
- Sugar: 0.09g
- Cholesterol: 178mg

Breaded Hake With Green Chili Pepper And Mayonnaise

Preparation time: 5 minutes. Cooking time: 20 minutes. Serve: 4

Ingredients:

- 4 breaded hake fillets
- Mayonnaise
- Green mojito
- Extra virgin olive oil

Direction:

1. Paint the breaded hake fillets with extra virgin olive oil.
2. Put them in the air fryer basket and select 180^0C, 30 minutes.
3. Meanwhile, put in a bowl 8 teaspoons of mayonnaise and 2 of green mojito. Both the mayonnaise and the green mojito can be homemade or commercial.
4. Let flirt well.
5. Serve the breaded hake fillets with the green mojito mayonnaise.

Nutrition Value (Nutrition per Serving):

- Calories: 132
- Fat: 4.38g
- Carbohydrates: 0.41g
- Protein: 21.38g
- Sugar: 0.09g
- Cholesterol: 178mg

Fried Anchovies

Preparation time: 5 minutes. Cooking time: 15 minutes. Serve: 4

Ingredients:

- 500g of anchovies
- Salt
- Flour
- Spray oil

Direction:

1. Clean the anchovies. You can, if you want, open in half, and remove the central spine.
2. Wash well, drain, and put salt.
3. Pass the anchovies for flour and place them in a large tray so that they are separated between them.
4. Spray with the oil canister so that the oil is well distributed by all of them.
5. Turn around and spray again with the oil.
6. Place the anchovies in the basket of the air fryer so that they are not on top of each other.
7. We select 180^0C, 15 minutes.
8. Do the same for a batch until you have all the fried anchovies.

Nutrition Value (Nutrition per Serving):

- Calories: 7
- Fat: 0.42g
- Carbohydrate: 0.01g
- Protein: 0.77g
- Sugar: 0g
- Cholesterol: 2mg

Roasted Peppers With Tuna Snacks

Preparation time: 5 minutes. Cooking time: 15 minutes. Serve: 4

Ingredients:

For tuna snacks:

- 3 cans of tuna in oil
- 1 clove garlic
- 1 tsp chopped parsley
- 3 tbsp grated cheese
- 1 tbsp fried tomato
- Salt and ground pepper
- 1 egg
- Breadcrumbs

For roasted peppers:

- 3 roasted red peppers
- 1 new onion
- Extra virgin olive oil
- Salt
- Vinegar

Direction:

1. Put in a bowl the tuna well drained with the egg, the finely chopped garlic, the parsley, the cheese, the fried tomato sauce, salt, and pepper.
2. Mix everything very well. Make small balls. Pass them through breadcrumbs. Put in the fridge. Put the peppers on a tray, put some threads of oil and salt. Take to the oven, 180^0C and roast on all their faces, turning occasionally, until they are roasted at all.
3. Let cool and peel. Cut the peppers into strips. Cut the new onion into fine julienne and mix with the peppers. Add oil, vinegar, and salt.
4. Place the tuna balls in the basket of the air fryer and select 15 minutes at 180^0C. Serve in each dish a base of roasted and seasoned peppers. On them place the tuna balls.

Nutrition Value (Nutrition per Serving):

- Calories: 340
- Fat: 25g
- Carbohydrate: 10g
- Protein: 16g
- Sugar: 0g
- Cholesterol: 9mg

Tuna, Egg And Mozzarella Patties

Preparation time: 5 minutes. Cooking time: 10 minutes. Serve: 4

Ingredients:

- 1 package of wafer wafers
- 1 can of tuna
- 1 or 2 cooked eggs
- 1 ball of fresh mozzarella
- Fried Tomato Sauce
- Oregano

Direction:

1. Drain the tuna and place it in a bowl.
2. Add the diced mozzarella and the egg cooked, peeled, and chopped.
3. Add a dash of tomato sauce and sprinkle oregano.
4. Let flirt well. The mixture should be thick.
5. Spread the filling between the wafers of patties and close.
6. Put in the basket of the air fryer, I get 6 in each goal.
7. Select 170^0C, 10 minutes.
8. When you have all the patties ready, serve.

Nutrition Value (Nutrition per Serving):

- Calories: 843.2
- Fat: 6.1g
- Carbohydrates: 32.1g
- Proteins: 4,5g
- Sugar: 0g
- Cholesterol: 27mg

Dye Fish With Tomato

Preparation time: 10 minutes. Cooking time: 50 minutes. Serve: 4

Ingredients:

- 8 dye fish
- 2 eggs
- Breadcrumbs
- Salt
- Ground pepper
- Homemade tomato sauce
- Extra virgin olive oil
- Potatoes

Direction:

1. Beat the eggs.
2. Season the dye fish.
3. Pass the fish through the beaten egg and then through the breadcrumbs.
4. Paint the breaded fillets with an oil brush and put them in the air fryer basket.
5. Select 180^0C, 20 minutes.
6. Meanwhile, make the tomato sauce in the Cuisine or in the Thermomix, at the beginning of the recipe, you have the links with the tomato sauce recipe in one or another machine.
7. Peel and put the potatoes in the air fryer, a little oil, salt and select 30 minutes.
8. Serve the fish fillets with the potatoes and a generous layer of tomato on top.

Nutrition Value (Nutrition per Serving):

- Calories: 130
- Fat: 4.5g
- Carbohydrates: 0g
- Protein: 21g
- Sugar: 0g
- Cholesterol: 0mg

Peppers Stuffed With Tuna

Preparation time: 10 minutes. Cooking time: 40 minutes. Serve: 4

Ingredients:

- 4 small roasting peppers
- 1 large can of tuna in oil
- 1 onion
- 1 zucchini
- 4 cloves of garlic
- Extra virgin olive oil
- Salt
- Ground pepper
- 2 or 3 eggs

Direction:

Put in a large pan a bottom of oil and add the chopped onion and zucchini. Sauté until tender and add the well-drained tuna.

Let flirt and splash.

Let the filling cool.

Beat the eggs and mix with the tuna filling.

Open the peppers by cutting the top and fill.

Place in the basket of the air fryer so that the filling does not come out.

Select 40 minutes, 180^0C. Control and if you see that they have set before, take them out or if you see that they need more time, leave a little more.

Nutrition Value (Nutrition per Serving):

- Calories: 68
- Fat: 2.8g
- Carbohydrates: 7g
- Protein: 3.1g
- Sugar: 3g
- Cholesterol: 0mg

Hake Loins In Tempura

Preparation time: 5 minutes. Cooking time: 20 minutes. Serve: 4

Ingredients:

- 4 hake loins
- 1 glass of beer
- Flour
- Salt
- Pepper
- Lemon
- Oil

Direction:

Put the hake loins in a bowl, salt and pepper and put some lemon juice.

Reserve in the freezer while you make the tempura. Put the cold beer in a bowl and add flour until a thick dough is obtained.

In one plate, put flour and in a flat source where the four loins separate from each other, put a thin layer of flour.

Pass a loin of hake through the flour of the plate, shake and dip in the tempura, let it drain a little and place it in the source where you have the thin layer of flour.

Do the same with all the loins.

Now sprinkle flour over the tempura.

Take the freezer for half an hour minimum.

What you do with these steps is that the tempura adheres to the hake loins for when you put them in the air fryer basket, it does not fall apart.

Put the loins carefully in the basket of the air fryer, spray with oil and select 180^0C, 20 minutes.

- Calories: 99
- Fat: 4.5g
- Carbohydrates: 1g
- Protein: 13.4g
- Sugar: 0g
- Cholesterol: 0mg

Cod Cakes

Preparation time: 5. Cooking time: 15 minutes. Serve: 4

Ingredients:

- Cod fritters
- Tomato
- Grated cheese

Direction:

1. Put the cod tortillas in the basket of the air fryer without stacking.
2. Select 180^0C, 15 minutes.
3. Take out and make another batch, so until you have all done.
4. Cut the tomato into slices.
5. Alternate a tomato slice with a cod omelet.
6. Top off with some grated cheese that will melt with the heat of the last cod pancake that you will place in the tower.

Nutrition Value (Nutrition per Serving):

- Calories: 227
- Fat: 13g
- Carbohydrates: 22g
- Protein: 4.9g
- Sugar: 2.2g
- Cholesterol: 0mg

Mackerel In Fried Marinade

Preparation time: 5 minutes. Cooking time: 20 minutes. Serve: 4

Ingredients:

- 4 medium mackerels
- Salt
- Ground pepper
- Half a glass of wine
- Half a glass of vinegar
- 1 tbsp cumin
- 1 tbsp oregano
- 1 tbsp paprika

Direction:

1. Clean the mackerels and chop.
2. Put on a tray and add the wine, vinegar, oregano, cumin and paprika and season. Stir well and leave 24 hours in the refrigerator.
3. Drain the mackerels.
4. Place in the bucket of the air fryer but without the pieces being piled up.
5. Select 20 minutes, 180^0C.
6. Take out and put another batch of mackerels.

Nutrition Value (Nutrition per Serving):

- Calories: 182
- Fats: 11.90g
- Carbohydrate: 0g
- Protein: 18.70g
- Sugar: 0g
- Cholesterol: 76mg

Fried Small Red Mullets

Preparation time: 10 minutes. Cooking time: 20 minutes. Serve: 2

Ingredients:

- 500g of small mullets
- Salt
- Ground pepper
- 1 glass of flour
- 1 glass of breadcrumbs
- Extra virgin olive oil

Direction:

1. Clean the mullets, remove scales, head, and guts.
2. Wash well and drain.
3. Season and put some oil threads.
4. Let bind well so that the oil is impregnated in all mullets.
5. In a bowl, put the flour next to the breadcrumbs and mix.
6. Pass the mullets through that flour linked with breadcrumbs.
7. Shake the excess and we are placing on the rack of the air fryer.
8. Select 180^0C about 15 to 20 minutes.
9. Shake the basket from time to time so that the mullets move and change position.

Nutrition Value (Nutrition per Serving):

- Calories: 90
- Fat: 3.7g
- Carbohydrates: 0g
- Proteins: 14,1g
- Sugar: 0g
- Cholesterol: 58mg

Fried Sardines

Preparation time: 10 minutes. Cooking time: 10 minutes. Serve: 4

Ingredients:

- 12 sardines
- Fishmeal
- Salt
- Extra virgin olive oil

Direction:

1. Clean the sardines, remove guts and if you want, the heads.
2. Put salt.
3. Pass the sardines for flour and shake well to remove the excess flour.
4. Put sardines, 4 in 4 or 6 in 6, in the air fryer basket, depending on the size. Do not pile up.
5. Spray with oil.
6. Close the drawer with the basket inside.
7. Select a high temperature, between 180^0C to 200^0C and about 10 minutes
8. At 10 minutes, shake the sardines and check if they are ready or need a few more minutes.
9. When they are golden brown to your liking, we take out. Continue with the next batch and so on until you finish.

Nutrition Value (Nutrition per Serving):

- Calories: 340
- Fat: 9.4g
- Carbohydrate: 0g
- Protein: 18g
- Sugar: 0g
- Cholesterol: 0mg

Crab Balls

Preparation time: 10 minutes. Cooking time: 20 minutes. Serve: 8

Ingredients:

- 250g of crab sticks
- 50g of crusty bread without crust
- 50g of cream cheese
- 50g of milk
- Salt
- Whipped egg and breadcrumbs
- Oil

Direction:

1. Put all the ingredients in the Thermomix glass.
2. Select 20 seconds speed 6.
3. Take the contents of the glass to a bowl and make small balls.
4. Pass the balls for breadcrumbs, then for beaten egg and again for breadcrumbs.
5. When you have them ready, place them in the air fryer basket and spray with extra virgin olive oil.
6. Put the basket in the drawer and put in the air fryer.
7. Select 160^0C, 10 minutes. Shake the basket so that the balls change position.
8. Select 180^0C, 10 minutes. Control so they don't brown too much.

Nutrition Value (Nutrition per Serving):

- Calories: 119
- Fat: 2.08g
- Carbohydrate: 0g
- Protein: 23.64g
- Sugar: 2.08g
- Cholesterol: 117mg

Fried Squid

Preparation time: 5 minutes. Cooking time: 13 minutes. Serve: 2

Ingredients:

- 2 Squids (body only, 150-200g)
- 1 tsp of wine
- ¼ tsp garlic powder
- 3 tsp flour
- A cup of breadcrumbs
- 1.5 tsp oil
- 1 tsp parsley powder
- 1 egg
- 1 tsp milk
- Pepper

For Tartar Sauce:

- ½ cup of mayonnaise
- 2 tsp chopped pickles
- 1 tsp chopped onion
- 1 tsp chopped capers
- 2 tsp mustard
- 1 tsp lemon juice
- 2-3 drops of chili pepper tabasco
- Salt
- Pepper

Direction:

1. Cut the clean squid into 1cm thick rings. Marine squid in white wine and garlic powder.
2. Mix the breadcrumbs with chopped parsley. Mix milk and pepper in beaten egg.
3. Pass the squid marinated in the flour, beaten egg and breadcrumbs respectively, and then place them in the frying dish.
4. Bake for 16-18 minutes in the air fryer at 180^0C. 6-8 minutes before the end of time, turn around, and then press the "Start" button to continue cooking.
5. Serve with tartar sauce.

Nutrition Value (Nutrition per Serving):

- Calories: 97
- Total Fat: 1.4g
- Carbohydrate: 0g
- Protein: 15.6g
- Sugar: 0g
- Cholesterol: 233mg

Fried Fish

Preparation time: 5 minutes. Cooking time: 15 minutes. Serve: 4

Ingredients:

- 300-900g Fresh fish fillets
- All types of fresh fish (except canned or breaded tuna) can be cooked whole or in fillets.

Direction:

1. Place the prepared fish in a dish smeared with butter.
2. Season with salt and pepper, sprinkle lemon juice and a little butter. Do not cover the plate.
3. Place the dish in the basket of the air fryer previously preheated for a few minutes at 180^0C.
4. Cook at 180^0C, in 15 minutes.

Nutrition Value (Nutrition per Serving):

- Calories: 84
- Protein: 17.76
- Fat: 0.92g
- Sugar: 0g
- Carbohydrates: 0g
- Cholesterol: 58mg

Breaded Shrimp

Preparation time: 5 minutes. Cooking time: 15 minutes. Serve: 4

Ingredients:

- 200g shrimp peeled and clean
- 2 tbsp starch
- Salt
- Pepper
- 1 egg white
- ½ cup breadcrumbs
- 1.5 tsp oil
- ¼ tsp paprika powder

Direction:

1. Peel the shrimp and remove moisture. Add salt and pepper to starch. Beat the egg white. Mix the breadcrumbs, oil, and paprika powder.
2. Preheat the air fryer at 180^0C for a few minutes.
3. Pair the shrimp with the mixture of starch, whipped egg white and breadcrumbs respectively, then place them in the frying pan.
4. Take to the fryer 180^0C for 11-13 minutes. 4-6 minutes before the end of time, turn around, then repeat the above process to continue cooking.

Nutrition Value (Nutrition per Serving):

- Calories: 130
- Fat: 14g
- Carbohydrates: 23g
- Protein: 13g
- Sugar: 0g
- Cholesterol: 134mg

Breaded Fish Fillet

Preparation time: 5 minutes. Cooking time: 20 minutes. Serve: 2

Ingredients:

- 300g of fish fillet
- Breadcrumbs
- Pepper salt to taste
- 2 tsp of oil

Direction:

1. Wash and remove the moisture from the fish, season with salt, pepper and breaded.
2. Preheat the air fryer at 180^0C for a few minutes.
3. Oil with the help of a brush.
4. Take to the fryer 180^0C for 17 minutes. 7 minutes before the time expires, flip the fish fillet, then press the "Start" button to continue cooking.

Nutrition Value (Nutrition per Serving):

- Calories: 42
- Fat: 2.25g
- Carbohydrate: 3.6g
- Protein: 1.88g
- Sugar: 0.42g
- Cholesterol: 5mg

Chapter 7: Vegan and Vegetarian Recipes

Homemade French Fries

Preparation time: 30 minutes. Cooking time: 28 minutes. Serve: 4

Ingredients:

- 2 reddish potatoes, cut into strips of 76 x 25 mm
- 1 liter of cold water, to soak the potatoes
- 15 ml of oil
- 3g garlic powder
- 2g of paprika
- Salt and pepper to taste
- Tomato sauce or ranch sauce, to serve

Direction:

1. Cut the potatoes into 76 x 25 mm strips and soak them in water for 15 minutes.
2. Drain the potatoes, rinse with cold, dry water with paper towels.
3. Add oil and spices to the potatoes, until they are completely covered.
4. Preheat the air fryer, set it to 195°C.
5. Add the potatoes to the preheated air fryer. Set the timer to 28 minutes.
6. Be sure to shake the baskets in the middle of cooking.
7. Remove the baskets from the air fryer when you have finished cooking and season the fries with salt and pepper.
8. Serve with tomato sauce or ranch sauce.

Nutrition Value (Nutrition per Serving):

- Calories: 390
- Fat: 36g
- Carbohydrates: 42g
- Protein: 5g
- Sugar: 4g
- Cholesterol: 0mg

Sweet Potato Chips

Preparation time: 5 minutes. Cooking time: 10 minutes. Serve: 4

Ingredients:

- 2 large sweet potatoes, cut into strips 25 mm thick
- 15 ml of oil
- 10g of salt
- 2g black pepper
- 2g of paprika
- 2g garlic powder
- 2g onion powder

Direction:

1. Cut the sweet potatoes into strips 25 mm thick.
2. Preheat the air fryer for a few minutes.
3. Add the cut sweet potatoes in a large bowl and mix with the oil until the potatoes are all evenly coated.
4. Sprinkle salt, black pepper, paprika, garlic powder and onion powder. Mix well.
5. Place the French fries in the preheated baskets and cook for 10 minutes at 205°C. Be sure to shake the baskets halfway through cooking.

Nutrition Value (Nutrition per Serving):

- Calories: 130
- Fat: 0g
- Carbohydrates: 29g
- Protein: 2g
- Sugar: 9g
- Cholesterol: 0mg

Cajun Style French Fries

Preparation time: 30 minutes. Cooking time: 28 minutes. Serve: 4

Ingredients:

- 2 reddish potatoes, peeled and cut into strips of 76 x 25 mm
- 1 liter of cold water
- 15 ml of oil
- 7g of Cajun seasoning
- 1g cayenne pepper
- Tomato sauce or ranch sauce, to serve

Direction:

1. Cut the potatoes into 76 x 25 mm strips and soak them in water for 15 minutes.
2. Drain the potatoes, rinse with cold, dry water with paper towels.
3. Preheat the air fryer, set it to 195°C.
4. Add oil and spices to the potatoes, until they are completely covered.
5. Add the potatoes to the preheated air fryer and set the timer to 28 minutes.
6. Be sure to shake the baskets in the middle of cooking
7. Remove the baskets from the air fryer when you have finished cooking and season the fries with salt and pepper.
8. Serve with tomato sauce or ranch sauce.

Nutrition Value (Nutrition per Serving):

- Calories: 156
- Fat: 8.01g
- Carbohydrate: 20.33g
- Protein: 1.98g
- Sugar: 0.33g
- Cholesterol: 0mg

Fried Zucchini

Preparation time: 10 minutes. Cooking time: 8 minutes. Serve: 4

Ingredients:

- 2 medium zucchinis, cut into strips 19 mm thick
- 60g all-purpose flour
- 12g of salt
- 2g black pepper
- 2 beaten eggs
- 15 ml of milk
- 84g Italian seasoned breadcrumbs
- 25g grated Parmesan cheese
- Nonstick Spray Oil
- Ranch sauce, to serve

Direction:

1. Cut the zucchini into strips 19 mm thick.
2. Mix with the flour, salt, and pepper on a plate. Mix the eggs and milk in a separate dish. Put breadcrumbs and Parmesan cheese in another dish.
3. Cover each piece of zucchini with flour, then dip them in egg and pass them through the crumbs. Leave aside.
4. Preheat the air fryer, set it to 175°C.
5. Place the covered zucchini in the preheated air fryer and spray with oil spray. Set the timer to 8 minutes and press Start / Pause.
6. Be sure to shake the baskets in the middle of cooking.
7. Serve with tomato sauce or ranch sauce.

Nutrition Value (Nutrition per Serving):

- Calories: 67
- Fat: 4.1g
- Carbohydrates: 4.5g
- Protein: 3.3g
- Sugar: 1.47g
- Cholesterol: 20.7mg

Fried Avocado

Preparation time: 15 minutes. Cooking time: 10 minutes. Serve: 2

Ingredients:

- 2 avocados cut into wedges 25 mm thick
- 50g Pan crumbs bread
- 2g garlic powder
- 2g onion powder
- 1g smoked paprika
- 1g cayenne pepper
- Salt and pepper to taste
- 60g all-purpose flour
- 2 eggs, beaten
- Nonstick Spray Oil
- Tomato sauce or ranch sauce, to serve

Direction:

1. Cut the avocados into 25 mm thick pieces.
2. Combine the crumbs, garlic powder, onion powder, smoked paprika, cayenne pepper and salt in a bowl.
3. Separate each wedge of avocado in the flour, then dip the beaten eggs and stir in the breadcrumb mixture.
4. Preheat the air fryer.
5. Place the avocados in the preheated air fryer baskets, spray with oil spray and cook at 205°C for 10 minutes. Turn the fried avocado halfway through cooking and sprinkle with cooking oil.
6. Serve with tomato sauce or ranch sauce.

Nutrition Value (Nutrition per Serving):

- Calories: 96
- Fat: 8.8g
- Sugar: 0.4g
- Carbohydrates: 5.12g
- Protein: 1.2g
- Cholesterol: 0mg

Vegetables In air Fryer

Preparation time: 20 minutes. Cooking time: 30 minutes. Serve: 2

Ingredients:

- 2 potatoes
- 1 zucchini
- 1 onion
- 1 red pepper
- 1 green pepper

Direction:

1. Cut the potatoes into slices.
2. Cut the onion into rings.
3. Cut the zucchini slices
4. Cut the peppers into strips.
5. Put all the ingredients in the bowl and add a little salt, ground pepper and some extra virgin olive oil.
6. Mix well.
7. Pass to the basket of the air fryer.
8. Select 160^0C, 30 minutes.
9. Check that the vegetables are to your liking.

Nutrition Value (Nutrition per Serving):

- Calories: 135
- Fat: 11g
- Carbohydrates: 8g
- Protein: 1g
- Sugar: 2g
- Cholesterol: 0mg

Crispy Rye Bread Snacks With Guacamole And Anchovies

Preparation time: 10 minutes. Cooking time: 10 minutes. Serve: 4

Ingredients:

- 4 slices of rye bread
- Guacamole
- Anchovies in oil

Direction:

1. Cut each slice of bread into 3 strips of bread.
2. Place in the basket of the air fryer, without piling up, and we go in batches giving it the touch you want to give it. You can select 180^0C, 10 minutes.
3. When you have all the crusty rye bread strips, put a layer of guacamole on top, whether homemade or commercial.
4. In each bread, place 2 anchovies on the guacamole.

Nutrition Value (Nutrition per Serving):

- Calories: 180
- Fat: 11.6g
- Carbohydrates: 16g
- Protein: 6.2g
- Sugar: 0g
- Cholesterol: 19.6mg

Mushrooms Stuffed With Tomato

Preparation time: 5 minutes. Cooking time: 50 minutes. Serve: 4

Ingredients:

- 8 large mushrooms
- 250g of minced meat
- 4 cloves of garlic
- Extra virgin olive oil
- Salt
- Ground pepper
- Flour, beaten egg and breadcrumbs
- Frying oil
- Fried Tomato Sauce

Direction:

1. Remove the stem from the mushrooms and chop it. Peel the garlic and chop. Put some extra virgin olive oil in a pan and add the garlic and mushroom stems.
2. Sauté and add the minced meat. Sauté well until the meat is well cooked and season.
3. Fill the mushrooms with the minced meat.
4. Press well and take the freezer for 30 minutes.
5. Pass the mushrooms with flour, beaten egg and breadcrumbs. Beaten egg and breadcrumbs.
6. Place the mushrooms in the basket of the air fryer.
7. Select 20 minutes, 180^0C.
8. Distribute the mushrooms once cooked in the dishes.
9. Heat the tomato sauce and cover the stuffed mushrooms.

Nutrition Value (Nutrition per Serving):

- Calories: 160
- Fat: 7.96g
- Carbohydrates: 19.41g
- Protein: 7.94g
- Sugar: 9.19g
- Cholesterol: 0mg

Spiced Potato Wedges

Preparation time: 15. Cooking time: 40 minutes. Serve 4

Ingredients:

- 8 medium potatoes
- Salt
- Ground pepper
- Garlic powder
- Aromatic herbs, the one we like the most
- 2 tbsp extra virgin olive oil
- 4 tbsp breadcrumbs or chickpea flour

Direction:

1. Put the unpeeled potatoes in a pot with boiling water and a little salt.
2. Let cook 5 minutes. Drain and let cool. Cut into thick segments, without peeling.
3. Put the potatoes in a bowl and add salt, pepper, garlic powder, the aromatic herb that we have chosen oil and breadcrumbs or chickpea flour.
4. Stir well and leave 15 minutes. Pass to the basket of the air fryer and select 20 minutes, 180^0C.
5. From time to time shake the basket so that the potatoes mix and change position. Check that they are tender.

Nutrition Value (Nutrition per Serving):

- Calories: 121
- Fat: 3g
- Carbohydrates: 19g
- Protein: 2g
- Sugar: 0g
- Cholesterol: 0mg

Egg Stuffed Zucchini Balls

Preparation time: 15 minutes. Cooking time: 45-60 minutes. Serve: 4

Ingredients:

- 2 zucchinis
- 1 onion
- 1 egg
- 120g of grated cheese
- 4 eggs
- Salt
- Ground pepper
- Flour

Direction:

1. Chop the zucchini and onion in the Thermomix, 10 seconds speed 8, in the Cuisine with the kneader chopper at speed 10 about 15 seconds or we can chop the onion by hand and the zucchini grate. No matter how you do it, the important thing is that the zucchini and onion are as small as possible.
2. Put in a bowl and add the cheese and the egg. Pepper and bind well.
3. Incorporate the flour, until you have a very brown dough with which you can wrap the eggs without problems.
4. Cook the eggs and peel.
5. Cover the eggs with the zucchini dough and pass through the flour.
6. Place the four balls in the basket of the air fryer and paint with oil.
7. Select 180^0C and leave for 45 to 60 minutes or until you see that the balls are crispy on the outside.
8. Serve over a layer of mayonnaise or aioli.

Nutrition Value (Nutrition per Serving):

- Calories: 23
- Fat: 0.5g
- Carbohydrates: 2g
- Protein: 1.8g
- Sugar: 0g
- Cholesterol: 15mg

Vegetables With Provolone

Preparation time: 10 minutes. Cooking time: 30 minutes. Serve: 4

Ingredients:

- 1 bag of 400g of frozen tempura vegetables
- Extra virgin olive oil
- Salt
- 1 slice of provolone cheese

Direction:

1. Put the vegetables in the basket of the air fryer. Add some strands of extra virgin olive oil and close.
2. Select 20 minutes, 200^0C.
3. Pass the vegetables to a clay pot and place the provolone cheese on top.
4. Take to the oven, 180^0C, about 10 minutes or so or until you see that the cheese has melted to your liking.

Nutrition Value (Nutrition per Serving):

- Calories: 104
- Fat: 8g
- Carbohydrates: 0g
- Protein: 8g
- Sugar: 0g
- Cholesterol: 0mg

Spicy Potatoes

Preparation time: 10 minutes. Cooking time: 30 minutes. Serve: 4

Ingredients:

- 400g potatoes
- 2 tbsp spicy paprika
- 1 tbsp olive oil
- Catupiry or cottage cheese
- Salt to taste

Direction:

1. Wash the potatoes with a brush. Unpeeled, cut vertically in a crescent shape, about 1 finger thick Place the potatoes in a bowl and cover with water. Let stand for about half an hour.
2. Preheat the air fryer. Set the timer of 5 minutes and the temperature to 200^0C.
3. Drain the water from the potatoes and dry with paper towels or a clean cloth. Put them back in the bowl and pour the oil, salt and paprika over them. Mix well with your hands so that all of them are covered evenly with the spice mixture. Pour the spiced potatoes in the basket of the air fryer. Set the timer for 30 minutes and press the power button. Stir the potatoes in half the time.
4. Remove the potatoes from the air fryer, place on a plate.
5. Serve with cheese and sauce.

Nutrition Value (Nutrition per Serving):

- Calories: 153
- Fat: 4g
- Carbohydrates: 26
- Protein: 3g
- Sugar: 0g
- Cholesterol: 5mg

Scrambled Eggs With Beans, Zucchini, Potatoes And Onions

Preparation time: 30 minutes. Cooking time: 35 minutes. Serve: 4

Ingredients:

- 300g of beans
- 2 onions
- 1 zucchini
- 4 potatoes
- 8 eggs
- Extra virgin olive oil
- Salt
- Ground pepper
- A splash of soy sauce

Direction:

1. Put the beans taken from their pod to cook in abundant saltwater. Drain when they are tender and reserve.
2. Peel the potatoes and cut into dice. Season and put some threads of oil. Mix and take to the air fryer. Select 180^0C, 15 minutes.
3. After that time, add together with the potatoes, diced zucchini, and onion in julienne, mix and select 180^0C, 20 minutes.
4. From time to time mix and stir.
5. Pass the contents of the air fryer together with the beans to a pan.
6. Add a little soy sauce and salt to taste.
7. Sauté and peel the eggs.
8. Do the scrambled.

Nutrition Value (Nutrition per Serving):

- Calories: 65
- Fat: 0.4g
- Carbohydrates: 8.6g
- Proteins: 4.6g
- Sugar: 0g
- Cholesterol: 0mg

French Toast

Preparation time: 5 minutes. Cooking time: 15 minutes. Serve: 8

Ingredients:

For the bread:

- 500g of flour
- 25g of oil
- 300 g of water
- 25g of fresh bread yeast
- 12g of salt

For French toast:

- Milk and cinnamon or milk and sweet wine
- Eggs
- Honey

Direction:

The first thing is to make bread a day before. Put in the MasterChef Gourmet the ingredients of the bread and knead 1 minute at speed 1. Let the dough rise 1 hour and knead 1 minute at speed 1 again. Remove the dough and divide into 4 portions. Make a ball and spread like a pizza. Roll up to make a small loaf of bread and let rise 1 hour or so.

Take to the oven and bake 40 minutes, 200^0C. Let the bread cool on a rack and reserve for the next day. Cut the bread into slices and reserve. Prepare the milk to wet the slices of bread. To do so, put the milk to heat, like 500 ml or so with a cinnamon stick or the same milk with a glass of sweet wine, as you like. When the milk has started to boil, remove from heat, and let cool.

Beat the eggs. Place a rack on a plate and we dip the slices of bread in the cold milk, then in the beaten egg and pass to the rack with the plate underneath to release the excess liquid. Put the slices of bread in the bucket of the air fryer, in batches, not piled up, and we take the air fryer, 180 degrees, 10 minutes each batch.

When you have all the slices passed through the air fryer, put the honey in a casserole, like 500g, next to 1 small glass of water and 4 tablespoons of sugar. When the honey starts to boil, lower the heat, and pass the bread slices through the honey. Place in a fountain and the rest of the honey we put it on top, bathing again the French toast. Ready our French toast, when they cool, they can already be eaten.

Nutrition Value (Nutrition per Serving):

- Calories: 224
- Fat: 15.2g
- Carbohydrates: 17.39g
- Protein: 4.81g
- Sugar: 5.76g
- Cholesterol: 84mg

Sweet Potato Salt And Pepper

Preparation time: 5 minutes. Cooking time: 20 minutes. Serve: 4

Ingredients:

- 1 large sweet potato
- Extra virgin olive oil
- Salt
- Ground pepper

Direction:

1. Peel the sweet potato and cut into thin strips, if you have a mandolin it will be easier for you.
2. Wash well and put salt.
3. Add a little oil to impregnate the sweet potato in strips and place in the air fryer basket.
4. Select 180^0C, 30 minutes or so. From time to time, shake the basket so that the sweet potato moves.
5. Pass to a tray or plate and sprinkle with fine salt and ground pepper.

Nutrition Value (Nutrition per Serving):

- Calories: 107
- Fat: 0.6g
- Carbohydrates: 24.19g
- Protein: 1.61g
- Sugar: 5.95g
- Cholesterol: 0mg

Potatoes With Provencal Herbs With Cheese

Preparation time: 5 minutes. Cooking time: 20 minutes. Serve: 4

Ingredients:

- 1kg of potatoes
- Provencal herbs
- Extra virgin olive oil
- Salt
- Grated cheese

Direction:

1. Peel the potatoes and cut the cane salt and sprinkle with Provencal herbs.
2. Put in the basket and add some strands of extra virgin olive oil.
3. Take the air fryer and select 180^0C, 20 minutes.
4. Take out and move on to a large plate.
5. Cover cheese.
6. Gratin in the microwave or in the oven, a few minutes until the cheese is melted.

Nutrition Value (Nutrition per Serving):

- Calories: 437
- Fat: 25g
- Carbohydrates: 42g
- Protein: 9g
- Sugar: 0g
- Cholesterol: 0mg

Potato Wedges

Preparation time: 3 minutes. Cooking time: 20 minutes. Serve: 4

Ingredients:

- 2 large thick potatoes, rinsed and cut into wedges 102 mm long
- 23 ml of olive oil
- 3g garlic powder
- 1g onion powder
- 3g of salt
- 1g black pepper
- 5g grated Parmesan cheese
- Tomato sauce or ranch sauce, for server

Direction:

1. Cut the potatoes into 102 mm long pieces.
2. Preheat the air fryer for 5 minutes. Set it to 195°C.
3. Cover the potatoes with olive oil and mix the condiments and Parmesan cheese until they are well covered.
4. Add the potatoes to the preheated fryer. Set the time to 20 minutes.
5. Be sure to shake the baskets in the middle of cooking.
6. Serve with tomato sauce or ranch sauce.

Nutrition Value (Nutrition per Serving):

- Calories: 156
- Fat: 8.01g
- Carbohydrate: 20.33g
- Protein: 1.98g
- Sugar: 0.33g
- Cholesterol: 0mg

Onion Rings

Preparation time: 10 minutes. Cooking time: 20 minutes. Serve: 2

Ingredients:

- 1 small white onion, cut into rounds 13 mm thick and separated into rings
- 84g crusty bread
- 2g smoked paprika
- 5g of salt
- 2 eggs
- 224 ml whey
- 60g all-purpose flour
- Nonstick Spray Oil

Direction:

1. Cut a sliced onion 13 mm thick and separate the layers into rings.
2. Combine breadcrumbs, paprika and salt in a bowl. Leave aside.
3. Beat eggs and buttermilk until completely mixed.
4. Dip each onion ring in the flour, then in the beaten eggs and finally in the breadcrumb mixture.
5. Preheat the air fryer, set it to 190°C.
6. Sprinkle the onion rings with cooking oil.
7. Place the onion rings in a single layer in the baskets of the preheated air fryer and cook in batches at 190°C for 10 minutes until golden brown. Be sure to use oil spray in the middle of cooking to cook evenly.
8. Serve with your favorite sauce.

Nutrition Value (Nutrition per Serving):

- Calories: 276
- Fat: 15.51g
- Carbohydrates: 31.32g
- Protein: 3.7g
- Sugar: 0g
- Cholesterol: 14mg

Onion Flower

Preparation time: 15 minutes. Cooking time: 25 minutes. Serve: 3

Ingredients:

- 1 large onion
- 120g all-purpose flour
- 7g of paprika
- 12g of salt
- 7g garlic powder
- 3g chili powder
- 1g black pepper
- 1g dried oregano
- 295 ml of water
- 56g Italian breadcrumbs
- Nonstick Spray Oil

Direction:

1. Peel the onion and cut the top. Place it on a cutting board. Cut down, from the center out on the cutting board. Repeat to create 8 evenly separated cuts around the onion. Make sure your cut goes through all the layers, but leave the onion connected in the center. Leave aside.
2. Cover the onion in cold water for at least 2 hours and then dry it. Put the flour, paprika, salt, garlic powder, chili powder, black pepper, oregano, and water until a mixture forms.
3. Preheat the air fryer for 5 minutes at 180^0C.
4. Cover the onion with the mixture, spreading it over the layers and making sure they are all covered. Then, sprinkle the top and bottom of the onion with the crumbs. Spray the bottom of the air fryer with cooking oil spray and place the onion inside cut up. Spray the top of the onion generously with oil spray.
5. Cook the onion at 205 ° C for 10 minutes, then cook for another 15 minutes at 175°C.

Nutrition Value (Nutrition per Serving):

- Calories: 120
- Fat: 9.02g
- Carbohydrate: 8.67g
- Protein: 1.72g
- Sugar: 3.76g
- Cholesterol: 16mg

Hasselback Potatoes

Preparation time: 3 minutes. Cooking time: 40 minutes. Serve: 2

Ingredients:

- 4 medium reddish potatoes washed and drained
- 30 ml of olive oil
- 12g of salt
- 1g black pepper
- 1g garlic powder
- 28g melted butter
- 8g parsley, freshly chopped, to decorate

Direction:

1. Wash and scrub potatoes. Let them dry with a paper towel.
2. Cut the slits, 6 mm away, on the potatoes, stopping before you cut them completely, so that all the slices are connected approximately 13 mm at the bottom of the potato.
3. Preheat the air fryer for 6 minutes, set it to 175°C.
4. Cover the potatoes with olive oil and season evenly with salt, black pepper, and garlic powder.
5. Add the potatoes in the air fryer and cook for 30 minutes at 175°C.
6. Brush the melted butter over the potatoes and cook for another 10 minutes at 175 ° C.
7. Garnish with freshly chopped parsley.

Nutrition Value (Nutrition per Serving):

- Calories: 415
- Fat: 42g
- Carbohydrate: 9g
- Protein: 1g

Roasted Potatoes

Preparation time: 3 minutes. Cooking time: 20 minutes. Serve: 4

Ingredients:

- 227g of small fresh potatoes, cleaned and halved
- 30 ml of olive oil
- 3g of salt
- 1g black pepper
- 2g garlic powder
- 1g dried thyme
- 1g dried rosemary

Direction:

1. Preheat the air fryer for a few minutes. Set it to 195°C.
2. Cover the potatoes in half with olive oil and mix the seasonings.
3. Place the potatoes in the preheated air fryer. Set the time to 20 minutes. Be sure to shake the baskets in the middle of cooking.

Nutrition Value (Nutrition per Serving):

- Calories: 93
- Fat: 0.13g
- Carbohydrates: 21.04g
- Protein: 2.49g
- Sugar: 1.g
- Cholesterol: mg

Honey Roasted Carrots

Preparation time: 5 minutes. Cooking time: 12 minutes. Serve: 2-4

Ingredients:

- 454g of rainbow carrots, peeled and washed
- 15 ml of olive oil
- 30 ml honey
- 2 sprigs of fresh thyme
- Salt and pepper to taste

Direction:

1. Wash the carrots and dry them with a paper towel. Leave aside.
2. Preheat the air fryer for a few minutes a 180^0C.
3. Place the carrots in a bowl with olive oil, honey, thyme, salt, and pepper. Place the carrots in the air fryer at 180^0C for 12 minutes. Be sure to shake the baskets in the middle of cooking.
4. Serve hot.

Nutrition Value (Nutrition per Serving):

- Calories: 125
- Fat: 7g
- Carbohydrates: 15.6g
- Protein: 1.2g
- Sugar: 8.6g
- Cholesterol: 0mg

Roasted Broccoli With Garlic

Preparation time: 3 minutes. Cooking time: 10 minutes. Serve 3

Ingredients:

- 1 large broccoli cut 5
- 15 ml of olive oil
- 3g garlic powder
- 3g of salt
- 1g black pepper

Direction:

1. Preheat the air fryer for 5 minutes. Set it to 150°C.
2. Sprinkle the broccoli pieces with olive oil and mix them until they are well covered.
3. Mix broccoli with seasonings.
4. Add the broccoli to the preheated air fryer at 150^0C for 5 minutes.

Nutrition Value (Nutrition per Serving):

- Calories: 278
- Fat: 5.1g
- Carbohydrates: 6.58g
- Proteins: 1.9g

Roasted Cauliflower

Preparation time: 2 minutes. Cooking time: 10 minutes. Serve: 2-3

Ingredients:

- 284g cauliflower
- 10 ml of olive oil
- 3g of salt
- 1g black pepper

Direction:

1. Preheat the air fryer, set it to 150°C.
2. Place the cauliflower florets in a container, sprinkle with olive oil and season with salt and pepper, covering the florets evenly.
3. Add the cauliflower to the preheated air fryer at 150^0C for 5 minutes.

Nutrition Value (Nutrition per Serving):

- Calories: 94
- Fat: 3.1g
- Carbohydrates: 15.4g
- Proteins: 4.5g
- Sugar: 0g
- Cholesterol: 0.0mg

Roasted Corn

Preparation time: 2 minutes. Cooking time: 10 minutes. Serve: 2

Ingredients:

- 1 ear of corn, with husks and silks removed, and cut in half
- 14g melted butter
- 2g of salt

Direction:

1. Preheat the air fryer for 3 minutes at 180^0C.
2. Pass the melted butter over the corn and season with salt.
3. Place the corn in the preheated air fryer at 180^0C for 7 minutes.
4. Be sure to shake the baskets in the middle of cooking.

Nutrition Value (Nutrition per Serving):

- Calories: 86
- Carbohydrates: 19g
- Fat: 1.2g
- Proteins: 3.2g

Roasted Pumpkin

Preparation time: 10 minutes. Cooking time: 12 minutes. Serve: 2-4

Ingredients:

- 1 pumpkin, peeled, seeded, and cut into 25 mm cubes
- 15 ml of olive oil, plus a little more to spray
- 1g of thyme leaves
- 6g of salt
- 1g black pepper

Direction:

1. Preheat the air fryer for a few minutes at 180^0C.
2. Cover the pumpkin cubes seasoned with olive oil and season with thyme, salt, and pepper.
3. Add seasoned squash to the preheated air fryer at 180^0C for 10 minutes.
4. Be sure to shake the baskets in the middle of cooking.
5. Sprinkle with olive oil when you finish cooking and serve.

Nutrition Value (Nutrition per Serving):

- Calories: 50.0
- Total Fat: 0.62g
- Carbohydrates: 10.81g
- Proteins: 2.48g

Roasted Eggplant

Preparation time: 5 minutes. Cooking time: 10 minutes. Serve: 1-2

Ingredients:

- 1 Japanese eggplant, sliced 13 mm thick
- 30 ml of olive oil
- 3g of salt
- 2g garlic powder
- 1g black pepper
- 1g onion powder
- 1g ground cumin

Direction:

1. Preheat the air fryer for 5 minutes at 180°C.
2. Cut the peeled eggplant into 13 mm thick slices.
3. Combine the oil and seasonings in a large bowl until well combined and mix the eggplant until all the pieces are well covered.
4. Place the eggplant in the preheated air fryer and cook at 205°C for 10 minutes.

Nutrition Value (Nutrition per Serving):

- Calories: 325
- Carbohydrates: 6.8g
- Fat: 4.2g
- Proteins: 1.9g
- Sugar: 3.5g
- Cholesterol: 0mg

Corn And Cheese Cakes

Preparation time: 8 minutes. Cooking time: 15 minutes. Serve: 6

Ingredients:

- 60g all-purpose flour
- 79g cornmeal
- 38g white sugar
- 6g of salt
- 7g baking powder
- 118 ml of milk
- 45g melted butter
- 1 egg
- 165g of corn
- 3 scallions, chopped
- 120g grated cheddar cheese
- Nonstick Spray Oil

Direction:

1. Put flour, cornmeal, sugar, salt, and baking powder in a bowl and mix everything.
2. Beat the milk, butter, and egg until well joined.
3. Mix the dry ingredients with the wet ingredients. Fold the corn, chives, and cheddar cheese.
4. Preheat the air fryer for 5 minutes. Set it to 160°C.
5. Grease the muffin molds with oil spray and place the mixture in the molds until they are a.
6. Add the muffins to the preheated air fryer at 180°C. Set the time to 15 minutes.
7. Serve the muffins with butter or enjoy them alone.

Nutrition Value (Nutrition per Serving):

- Calories: 35
- Fat: 0.2g
- Carbohydrates: 7.5g
- Protein: 0.7g
- Sugar: 2.1g
- Cholesterol: 0mg

Chapter 8: Desserts

Sweet Sponge Cake

Preparation time: 15 minutes. Cooking time: 60 minutes. Serve: 10

Ingredients:

- 250g baking powder with yeast
- 250g of sugar
- 3 medium eggs
- 3 tbsp olive oil Grated orange
- 300g chopped pistachio
- 1 sachet of yeast
- Lemon cream:
- 1 egg white
- 150g luster sugar
- 100 ml sour cream
- 1 tsp lemon juice

Direction:

1. Separate the yolks from the eggs. Mount the egg whites until stiff with the blender and gradually incorporate the sugar. Mix until you get a thick white cream. Apart, beat the yolks with the oil and orange zest.

2. Incorporate this mixture with the clear ones, mix in an enveloping way and finally incorporate the flour and the yeast with a sieve. When everything is well mixed, add the pistachios. You can use a circular mold greased with oil and flour or kitchen paper that is more comfortable.

3. Add the cake dough to the mold. Preheat the air fryer a few minutes to 160^0C. Insert the mold into the basket of the air fryer and set the timer for about 30 minutes at 160°C. While it is cooked prepare the lemon cream.

4. To do so, gradually mix the white with the sugar, add the lemon juice and add Sour cream and mix until you get a thick cream. Serve the sponge cake with the lemon cream on top and sprinkle with chopped pistachios.

Nutrition Value (Nutrition per Serving):

- Calories: 495
- Fat: 23g
- Carbohydrates: 62g
- Protein: 10g
- Sugar: 300g
- Cholesterol: 67mg

Egg Flan

Preparation time: 15 minutes. Cooking time: 60 minutes. Serve: 4

Ingredients:

- 300 ml of milk
- 3 eggs
- 80g of sugar

Direction:

Put the sugar in a saucepan reserving two tablespoons for later. Add some water. With very low heat melt the sugar until everything is liquid and caramelized.

Immediately pour into the molds for custards (whether they are individual or if it is a large flan). It is important to do it right away because the caramel solidifies very quickly when it cools.

In a separate bowl, beat the eggs with the help of some rods. When they begin to foam, add the milk, and mix everything very well.

Once the mixture is homogeneous pour into the molds to which we have previously put the candy.

Next, preheat the air fryer a few minutes to 160^0C. Then cook the custards in a water bath in the Ai fryer. To do so, arrange the flan inside the basket of the air fryer in a container with water ensuring that water reaches half of the containers but ensuring that no water enters them.

Put the bowl with the custards and with the water half by bathing them in the air fryer and let everything cook at medium temperature 160 C for about 1 hour.

To check if the custards are cooked, shake gently and if, when moving, they have the consistent appearance of the custards, they are ready. Otherwise, if they look very liquid, bake them in the water bath a little more.

Nutrition Value (Nutrition per Serving):

- Calories: 175
- Fat: 6g
- Carbohydrates: 24g
- Protein: 7g
- Sugar: 80g
- Cholesterol: 160mg

Roasted Apples

Preparation time: 10 minutes. Cooking time: 20 minutes. Serve: 4

Ingredients:

- 4 apples
- 4 tsp butter
- 4 tsp honey
- A little cinnamon powder

Direction:

Separate apples to remove the shape of the heart.

Incorporate, in the center of each apple, a teaspoon of butter, another of honey and a little cinnamon.

Preheat the air fryer a few minutes at 180^0C.

Put the apples in the basket of the air fryer and set the timer 20 minutes at 180^0C

Nutrition Value (Nutrition per Serving):

- Calories: 179
- Fat: 11g
- Carbohydrates: 20g
- Protein: 0g
- Sugar: 50g
- Cholesterol: 31mg

Homemade Muffins

Preparation time: 10 minutes. Cooking time: 15 minutes. Serve 3

Ingredients:

- 6 tbsp olive oil
- 100g of sugar
- 2 eggs
- 100g flour
- 1 tsp Royal baking powder
- Lemon zest

Direction:

1. Beat the eggs with the sugar, with the help of a whisk. Add the oil little by little, while stirring, until you get a fluffy cream.
2. Then add the lemon zest.
3. Finally, add the sifted flour with the yeast to the previous mixture and mix in an envelope.
4. Fill 2/3 of the muffin muffins with the dough.
5. Preheat the air fryer a few minutes to 180^0C and when ready place the muffins in the basket.
6. Set the timer for approximately 20 minutes at a temperature of 180^0C, until they are golden brown.

Nutrition Value (Nutrition per Serving):

- Calories: 240
- Fat: 12g
- Carbohydrates: 29g
- Protein: 4g
- Sugar: 100g
- Cholesterol: 67g

Palm Trees Hojaldre

Preparation time: 5 minutes. Cooking time: 15 minutes. Serve: 2

Ingredients:

- 1 Sheet of puff pastry
- Sugar

Direction:

1. Stretch the puff pastry sheet.
2. Pour the sugar over and fold the puff pastry sheet in half.
3. Put a thin layer of sugar on top and fold the puff pastry in half again.
4. Roll the puff pastry sheet from both ends towards the center (creating the shape of the palm tree).
5. Cut into sheets 5-8 mm thick.
6. Preheat the air fryer to 180^0C and put the palm trees in the basket.
7. Set the timer about 10 minutes at 180^0C.

Nutrition Value (Nutrition per Serving):

- Calories: 317
- Fat: 17g
- Carbohydrates: 38g
- Protein: 3g
- Sugar: 40g
- Cholesterol: 23g

Chocolate And Nut Cake

Preparation time: 10 minutes. Cooking time: 30 minutes. Serve: 4

Ingredients:

- 60g dark chocolate
- 2 butter spoons
- 1 egg
- 3 spoonful's of sugar
- 50g flour
- 1 envelope Royal yeast
- Chopped walnuts

Direction:

1. Melt the dark chocolate with the butter, over low heat. Once melted, put in a bowl.
2. Incorporate the egg, sugar, flour, yeast (the latter passed through the sieve, to prevent lumps from forming) and finally the chopped nuts.
3. Beat well by hand until you get a uniform dough.
4. Put the dough in a silicone mold or oven suitable for incorporation in the basket of the air fryer.
5. Preheat the air fryer a few minutes at 180^0C.
6. Set the timer for 20 minutes at 180^0C and when it has cooled down, unmold.

Nutrition Value (Nutrition per Serving):

- Calories: 108
- Fat: 4g
- Carbohydrates: 16g
- Protein: 2g
- Sugar: 250g
- Cholesterol: 3mg

Light Cheese Cake With Strawberry Syrup

Preparation time: 10 minutes. Cooking time: 20 minutes. Serve: 4

Ingredients:

- 500g cottage cheese
- 3 whole eggs
- 2 tbsp powdered sweetener
- 2 tbsp oat bran
- ½ tbsp baking yeast
- 2 tbsp cinnamon
- 2 tbsp vanilla aroma
- 1 lemon (the skin)

Direction:

1. Mix in a bowl the cottage cheese, the sweetener, the cinnamon, the vanilla aroma, and the lemon zest. Mix very well until you get a homogeneous cream.
2. Incorporate the eggs one by one.
3. Finally, add oats and yeast mixing well.
4. Put the whole mixture in a container to fit in the air fryer.
5. Preheat the air fryer a few minutes at 180^0C.
6. Insert the mold into the basket of the air fryer and set the timer for about 20 minutes at 180°C.

Nutrition Value (Nutrition per Serving):

- Calories: 191
- Fat: 9g
- Carbohydrates: 21g
- Protein: 4g
- Sugar: 18g
- Cholesterol: 0mg

Banana And Nut Bread

Preparation time: 10 minutes. Cooking time: 40 minutes. Serve: 1

Ingredients:

- 28g unsalted butter, softened
- 100g of sugar
- 1 egg, beaten
- 2 ripe mashed bananas
- 2 ml of pure vanilla extract
- 20g all-purpose flour
- 3g baking soda
- 2g salt
- 40g chopped walnuts
- Nonstick Spray Oil

Direction:

1. Mix the butter with the sugar.
2. Mix the eggs, mashed bananas, and vanilla. Set aside
3. Preheat the air fryer for a few minutes and set the temperature to 150°C.
4. Sift flour, baking soda and salt.
5. Join the dry ingredients in the moist ones until they combine. Then mix the chopped nuts.
6. Grease 1 mold for mini breads with oil spray and fill it with the mixture. Place in the preheated air fryer. Set to 40 minutes.

Nutrition Value (Nutrition per Serving):

- Calories: 285
- Fat: 11g
- Carbohydrates: 38g
- Protein: 5g
- Sugar: 20g
- Cholesterol: 11mg

Apple Mini Cakes

Preparation time: 35 minutes. Cooking time: 10 minutes. Serve: 2

Ingredients:

- 1 medium apple, peeled and diced, into bite-sized pieces
- 18g granulated sugar
- 18g unsalted butter
- 2g ground cinnamon
- 1g ground nutmeg
- 1g ground allspice
- 1 sheet prefabricated cake dough
- 1 beaten egg
- 5 ml of milk

Direction:

1. Put diced apples, granulated sugar, butter, cinnamon, nutmeg, and allspice in a medium saucepan or in a skillet over medium-low heat.
2. Simmer for 2 minutes and remove from heat.
3. Allow the apples to cool, discovered at room temperature for 30 minutes.
4. Cut the cake dough into circles of 127 mm.
5. Add the filling to the center of each circle and use your finger to apply water to the outer ends. Some filler will be left unused.
6. Close the cake cut a small opening at the top.
7. Preheat the air fryer for a few minutes and set the temperature to 175°C.
8. Mix the eggs and milk and spread the mixture on each foot.
9. Place the cakes in the preheated air fryer and cook at 175°C for 10 minutes until the cakes are golden brown.

Nutrition Value (Nutrition per Serving):

- Calories: 331
- Fat: 15.6g
- Carbohydrates: 46.4g
- Protein: 3g
- Sugar: 0g
- Cholesterol: 0mg

Rustic Pear Pie With Nuts

Preparation time: 1h 10 minutes. Cooking time: 45 minutes. Serve: 4

Ingredients:

Cake:

- 100g all-purpose flour
- 1g of salt
- 12g granulated sugar
- 84g unsalted butter, cold, cut into 13 mm pieces
- 30 ml of water, frozen
- 1 egg, beaten
- 12g turbinated sugar
- Nonstick Spray Oil
- 20g of honey
- 5 ml of water
- Roasted nuts, chopped, to decorate

Filling:

- 1 large pear, peeled, finely sliced
- 5g cornstarch
- 24g brown sugar
- 1g ground cinnamon
- A pinch salt

Direction:

1. Mix 90 g of flour, salt, and granulated sugar in a large bowl until well combined. Join the butter in the mixture using a pastry mixer or food processor until thick crumbs form. Add cold water and mix until it joins. Shape the dough into a bowl, cover with plastic and let cool in the refrigerator for 1 hour.

2. Mix the stuffing ingredients in a bowl until they are combined. Roll a roll through your cooled dough until it is 216 mm in diameter. Add 10 g of flour on top of the dough leaving 38 mm without flour. Place the pear slices in decorative circles superimposed on the floured part of the crust. Remove any remaining pear juice on the slices. Fold the edge over the filling.

3. Cover the edges with beaten eggs and sprinkle the sugar over the whole cake. Set aside

4. Preheat the air fryer set the temperature to 160°C. Spray the preheated air fryer with oil spray and place the cake inside. Set the time to 45 minutes at 160^0C. Mix the honey and water and pass the mixture through the cake when you finish cooking.

5. Garnish with toasted chopped nuts.

Nutrition Value (Nutrition per Serving):

- Calories: 20
- Fat: 0g
- Carbohydrates: 0g
- Protein: 0g
- Sugar: 0g
- Cholesterol: 0mg

Lemon Biscuit

Preparation time: 20 minutes. Cooking time: 30 minutes. Serve: 1

Ingredients:

- 120g all-purpose flour
- 4g baking powder
- A pinch of salt
- 84g unsalted butter, softened
- 130g granulated sugar
- 1 large egg
- 15g of fresh lemon juice
- 1 lemon, lemon zest
- 56g whey

Direction:

1. Mix the flour, baking powder and salt in a bowl. Set aside. Add the softened butter to an electric mixer and beat until soft and fluffy. Approximately 3 minutes Beat the sugar in the butter for 1 minute. Beat the flour mixture in the butter until it is completely united, for about 1 minute.

2. Add the egg, lemon juice and lemon zest. Mix until everything is completely united. Slowly pour the whey while mixing at medium speed. Add the mixture to a tray of greased mini loaves on top.

3. Preheat the air fryer set the temperature to 160°C.

4. Place the cake in the preheated air fryer. Set the time to 30 minutes at 160°C.

Nutrition Value (Nutrition per Serving):

- Calories: 403
- Fat: 22g
- Carbohydrates: 48g
- Protein: 5g
- Sugar: 0g
- Cholesterol: 0mg

Cranberry And Lemon Muffins

Preparation time: 10 minutes. Cooking time: 15 minutes. Serve: 6-8

Ingredients:

- 5 ml of lemon juice
- 112g of coconut milk or soymilk
- 120g all-purpose flour
- 4g baking powder
- 2g of baking soda
- 1g of salt
- 50g granulated sugar
- 60 ml coconut oil, liquid
- 1 lemon, lemon zest
- 5 ml vanilla extract
- 75g of fresh blueberries
- Nonstick Spray Oil

Direction:

1. Put the lemon juice and coconut milk in a small bowl and then set the mixture aside. Mix the flour, baking powder, baking soda and salt in a separate bowl and set aside. Mix the sugar, coconut oil, lemon zest and vanilla extract in an additional bowl. Then, combine with the coconut-lemon mixture and stir to combine.
2. Mix the dry ingredients to the wet ones gradually, until the mixture is smooth. Gently place the blueberries.
3. Preheat the air fryer for 5 minutes and set the temperature to 150°C.
4. Grease the muffin molds with oil spray and pour the mixture until the cups are ¾.
5. Place the muffin molds carefully in the preheated air fryer. Set the timer to 15 minutes at 150°C.
6. Remove the muffins when you finish cooking and let them cool for 10 minutes. Then serve them.

Nutrition Value (Nutrition per Serving):

- Calories: 215
- Fat: 9g
- Carbohydrates: 30.8g
- Protein: 2.6g
- Sugar: 18.7g
- Cholesterol: 17.1 mg

Espresso Chocolate Muffins

Preparation time: 10 minutes. Cooking time: 15 minutes. Serve 8

Ingredients:

- 120g all-purpose flour
- 60g cocoa powder
- 150g light brown sugar
- 2g baking powder
- 2g espresso coffee powder
- 3g of baking soda
- 1g of salt
- 1 large egg
- 170 ml of milk
- 5 ml vanilla extract
- 5 ml apple cider vinegar
- 80 ml of vegetable oil
- Nonstick Spray Oil

Direction:

1. Mix the flour, cocoa powder, sugar, baking powder, espresso coffee powder, baking soda and salt in a large bowl.
2. Beat the egg, milk, vanilla, vinegar, and oil in a separate bowl.
3. Mix the wet ingredients in the dry ones until they are well combined.
4. Grease the muffin pans with oil spray and pour the mixture until they are filled to ¾.
5. Preheat the air fryer for a few minutes and set the temperature to 150°C.
6. Place the muffin molds carefully in the preheated air fryer. You may have to work in parts.
7. Put the muffins in the air fryer previously preheated and set the time to 15 minutes at 150°C.

Nutrition Value (Nutrition per Serving):

- Calories: 374
- Fat: 17.31g
- Carbohydrates: 48.86g
- Protein: 9.41g
- Sugar: 7.73
- Cholesterol: 45g

Coconut Macaroni

Preparation time: 10 minutes. Cooking time: 15 minutes. Serve: 5-6

Ingredients:

- 100g of sweetened condensed milk
- 1 egg white
- 2 ml almond extract
- 2 ml vanilla extract
- A pinch of salt
- 175g unsweetened and shredded coconut

Direction:

1. Mix the condensed milk, egg white, almond extract, and salt in a bowl.
2. Add 160g of grated coconut and mix until well combined. The mixture must be able to maintain its shape.
3. Form 38 mm balls with your hands. In a separate dish, add 25 g of grated coconut.
4. Roll the coconut macaroni in the grated coconut until they are covered.
5. Preheat the air fryer for a few minutes and set the temperature to 150°C.
6. Add the coconut macaroni to the preheated air fryer. Set the time to 15 minutes at 150°C.
7. Let the macaroni cool for 5-10 minutes and serve when they finish cooling.

Nutrition Value (Nutrition per Serving):

- Calories: 35
- Fat: 2g
- Carbohydrate: 3g
- Protein: 1g
- Sugar: 40g
- Cholesterol: 0mg

Cranberry And Orange Muffins

Preparation time: 10 minutes. Cooking time: 15 minutes. Serve: 6-8

Ingredients:

- 120g all-purpose flour
- 66g of sugar
- 4g baking powder
- 2g of baking soda
- A pinch salt
- 100g of blueberries
- 1 egg
- 80 ml of orange juice
- 60 ml of vegetable oil
- 1 orange, zest
- Nonstick Spray Oil

Direction:

1. Mix the flour, baking powder, baking soda, salt, and blueberries in a large bowl.
2. Beat the egg, orange juice, oil, and orange zest in a separate bowl.
3. Mix the wet and dry ingredients until well combined.
4. Grease the muffin pans with oil spray and pour the mixture until they are filled to ¾.
5. Preheat the air fryer for a few minutes and set the temperature to 150°C.
6. Place the muffin molds carefully in the preheated air fryer. You may have to work in parts. Set the time to 15 minutes at 150°C.

Nutrition Value (Nutrition per Serving):

- Calories: 215
- Fat: 9g
- Carbohydrates: 30.8g
- Protein: 2.6g
- Sugar: 18.7g
- Cholesterol: 17.1 mg

Chocolate Chip Muffins

Preparation time: 10 minutes. Cooking time: 15 minutes. Serve: 6-8

Ingredients:

- 50g granulated sugar
- 125 ml of coconut milk or soymilk
- 60 ml coconut oil, liquid
- 5 ml vanilla extract
- 120g all-purpose flour
- 14g cocoa powder
- 4g baking powder
- 2g of baking soda
- A pinch of salt
- 85g chocolate chips
- 25g of pistachios, cracked (optional)
- Nonstick Spray Oil

Direction:

1. Put the sugar, coconut milk, coconut oil and vanilla extract in a small bowl, then set aside. Mix the flour, cocoa powder, baking powder, baking soda and salt in a separate bowl and set aside.
2. Mix the dry ingredients with the wet ingredients gradually, until smooth. Then join with the chocolate and pistachio.
3. Preheat the air fryer for a few minutes and set the temperature to 150°C. Grease the muffin pans with oil spray and pour the mixture until they are filled to ¾.
4. Place the muffin molds carefully in the preheated air fryer. Set the time to 15 minutes at 150°C.
5. Remove the muffins when finished cooking and let them cool for 10 minutes before serving.

Nutrition Value (Nutrition per Serving):

- Calories: 374
- Fat: 17.31g
- Carbohydrates: 48.86g
- Protein: 9.41g
- Sugar: 7.73
- Cholesterol: 45g

Cookies

Preparation time: 5 minutes. Cooking time: 12 minutes. Serve: 10

Ingredients:

- ½ cup muscovado sugar
- 1 egg
- ¾ cup of sugar tea
- 1 tsp of baking powder tea
- 1 tsp vanilla extract tea
- 1 and ¾ cup wheat flour
- 100g butter at room temperature
- ½ cup flaked oat tea
- 300g chopped nuts or chestnuts

Direction:

1. In a bowl, mix the butter, sugar, muscovado sugar and oatmeal by hand. Add vanilla essence. Beat the egg in a bowl and gradually add in income. Mix well. Add the flour gradually to form homogeneous dough. Add the yeast and mix again. Stretch the dough on a flat surface and add the nuts.

2. Mix by hand until they remain homogeneous. Make balls about 3 cm in diameter, place on a baking sheet and place in the freezer for an hour. Cover the bottom of the basket of the air fryer with aluminum foil. Preheat the air fryer. Set the timer of 5 minutes and the temperature to 200^0C.

3. Place six cookies in the basket leaving space between them and set the timer to 6 minutes and press the power button. When you have finished cooking, carefully remove with the help of a spatula, because cookies are still soft. Place on a clean and flat surface. Serve hot.

Nutrition Value (Nutrition per Serving):

- Calories: 189
- Fat: 10g
- Carbohydrates: 22g
- Protein: 1g
- Sugar: 14g
- Cholesterol: 0mg

Chocolate Churros

Preparation time: 5 minutes. Cooking time: 20 minutes. Serve: 16

Ingredients:

- 2 cups of water
- 2 tbsp sugar
- 1 tsp salt coffee
- 1 tbsp oil
- 2 cups flour
- 2 tbsp chocolate powder soup
- ½ cup of sugar mixed with 1 level scoop of cinnamon powder to sprinkle
- Sweet milk to fill

Direction:

1. In a bowl put the water, sugar, salt, and oil. Bring to a high heat until it boils. When it boils, pour the flour mixed with the chocolate once it is still on the fire and mix quickly with a wooden spoon until the dough remains homogeneous. Turn off the heat and let the dough cool.
2. Place the dough still hot in a churros machine and model them with about 6 cm in length and brush with oil. Reserve. If you do not have a churros machine, use a pastry bag with a more open beak, but you will not be left with the hole in the center to fill.
3. Preheat the air fryer. Set the time of 5 minutes and the temperature to 200^0C.
4. Place half of the churros in the basket of the air fryer and set the time to 15 minutes and press the power button. Turn in half the time. Still hot, pass them in the sugar and cinnamon mixture and then fill with the sweet.

Nutrition Value (Nutrition per Serving):

- Calories: 111
- Fat: 6.86g
- Carbohydrate: 11.76g
- Protein: 0.77g
- Sugar: 6.18g
- Cholesterol: 7mg

Roasted Banana

Preparation time: 5 minutes. Cooking time: Serve: 2

Ingredients:

- 1 tbsp butter
- 2 medium bananas
- 1 spoon of sugar
- 1 tbsp cinnamon coffee
- 1 squeezed orange

Direction:

1. Cover the bottom of the basket of the air fryer with aluminum foil and let the edges very high as the recipe will form a broth that should be used. If you prefer, use a refractory that fits in the basket of the air fryer. Preheat the air fryer.
2. Set the time of 5 minutes and the temperature to 200^0C. At the end of the time the air fryer will turn off.
3. Place the pieces of butter in the foil or refractory. Place the bananas cut in half. Set the time of the air fryer for 4 minutes and press the power button.
4. Remove the basket and convert the bananas. Add the orange juice. Set the time for 4 minutes and press the power button.
5. Transfer for a dish with broth that will form. Sprinkle with sugar mixed with cinnamon and serve still hot.

Nutrition Value (Nutrition per Serving):

- Calories: 276
- Fat: 0.43g
- Carbohydrate: 74.3g
- Protein: 1.87g
- Sugar: 33.38g
- Cholesterol: 0mg

Cupcake

Preparation time: 15 minutes. Cooking time: 17 minutes. Serve: 12

Ingredients:

- 2 eggs
- 1 cup of sugar tea
- 1 cup flour tea
- ½ cup of tea with milk
- 2 tbsp melted butter
- ½ tsp of baking powder
- 12 silicone or aluminum molds greased with margarine
- 1 cup icing sugar
- 2 tbsp warm water
- Chocolate counts to decorate

Direction:

1. Preheat the air fryer. Set the time of 5 minutes and the temperature to 200^0C.

2. Mix all ingredients except yeast in your Blender. Add the yeast stirring gently. Fill 2/3 of each mold the dough.

3. Place 6 individual molds in the basket of the air fryer. Set the time of 12 minutes and press the power button. In half the time, check to accompany if the cupcakes are already with the golden surface and cooked inside. If necessary, adjust the preparation time. To verify a toothpick sticks and if it has dried, the cupcake is ready. Remove the molds with the help of a spatula and repeat with the other 6 individual molds.

4. Slowly add the hot water to a stirring icing sugar quickly to form a thick paste. Cover the cupcakes with frosting and decorate to your liking.

Nutrition Value (Nutrition per Serving):

- Calories: 227
- Fat: 10.93g
- Carbohydrate: 29.77g
- Protein: 3.03g
- Sugar: 14.6g
- Cholesterol: 31g

Petit Gateau

Preparation time: 15 minutes. Cooking time: 15 minutes. Serve: 12

Ingredients:

- 200g semi-sweet chocolate
- 2 butter spoons
- 1 spoon of sugar
- 2 tbsp wheat flour
- 2 eggs
- 2 egg yolks
- Chocolate powder to sprinkle
- 12 silicone or aluminum molds dusted with cocoa powder

Direction:

1. Preheat the air fryer. Set the time of 5 minutes and the temperature to 200^0C.
2. Beat the eggs and egg yolks with the sugar in the blender until they are very clear. Add the chocolate and the melted flour, mixing with a spatula. Fill 2/3 of each mold with the dough.
3. Place 6 individual molds in the basket of the air fryer. Set the time of seven minutes in silicone molds and metal molds 8 to 10 minutes and press the power button. In half the time, check to accompany if they are already with the golden surface. The Petit gateau should not be fully baked so that the chocolate melted in the center. Remove the molds with the help of a spatula and repeat with the other 6 individual molds.
4. Unmold still hot with the help of a knife and place directly on a deep plate. It must be accompanied with vanilla ice cream and chocolate syrup.

Nutrition Value (Nutrition per Serving):

- Calories: 807
- Fat: 37g
- Carbohydrates: 110g
- Protein: 8
- Sugar: 0g
- Cholesterol: 0mg

Mini Cream Pump

Preparation time: 15 minutes. Cooking time: 15 minutes. Serve: 24

Ingredients:

- 1 cup water
- 2 tbsp sugar
- ½ tsp salt tea
- 1/3 cup margarine or butter
- 1 cup of flour
- 2 whole eggs
- 1 essence of the coffee spoon
- Vanilla cream
- 1 can of condensed milk
- 2 egg yolks
- 3 tbsp cornstarch
- Ice formation
- 1 cup sugar
- 2 tbsp warm water

Direction:

1. Preheat the air fryer. Set the time of 5 minutes and the temperature to 200^0C. In a saucepan put the water, sugar, salt, margarine or butter, place over high heat until it boils. Once it starts to boil the flour is poured at a time, turn off the heat and stir constantly until it is well consistent. Transfer the dough to a bowl, and add the lightly beaten vanilla eggs, shake vigorously until smooth dough.

2. Pass the dough in a pastry bag and make balls of 3 cm each already inside the basket of the air fryer. Set the airtime 10 minutes and press the power button. Mix the condensed milk, egg yolks and cornstarch in a saucepan over low heat until it thickens constantly stirring with a wire whisk. After vigorously stiff shaking cool slightly.

3. Remove the mini pumps of frying air fryer with the help of tweezers and let cool. Cut them in half and fill with the cream.

4. Slowly add the hot water to a stirring powdered sugar quickly to form a thick paste. Cover the top of the mini cream pumps with this frosting.

Nutrition Value (Nutrition per Serving):

- Calories: 326.08
- Fat: 10.87g
- Hydrates: 48.34g
- Proteins: 8.7g
- Sugar: 7.91g
- Cholesterol: 0mg

Brownies

Preparation time: 15 minutes. Cooking time: 45 minutes. Serve: 4

Ingredients:

- 150g butter
- 90g dark chocolate
- 300g of sugar
- 150g flour
- 1 tsp baking powder
- 2 tsp vanilla
- 3 eggs

Direction:

1. Chop the chocolate and melt in a saucepan over low heat.
2. Mix the flour with the baking powder.
3. Mix the butter with the sugar until it melts, then the eggs, the flour, vanilla, and chocolate.
4. Bone the mold with butter, place the preparation on top
5. Cook in a preheated air fryer at 160°C for 40 minutes.

Nutrition Value (Nutrition per Serving):

- Calories: 129
- Fat: 4.68g
- Carbohydrate: 21.26g
- Protein: 1.62g
- Sugar: 12.5f
- Cholesterol: 12mg

Apple Pie

Preparation time: 110 minutes. Cooking time: 30 minutes. Serve: 10

Ingredients:

- 3 green or golden apples
- 200 ml Syrup (100g Sugar + 200g Water)
- 2 tbsp sugar
- 1 puff pastry
- Peach jam

- 50g of sugar
- 250 ml of milk
- 2 egg yolks
- 20g cornstarch
- A little cinnamon
- 1 lemon
- Vanilla

For the custard:

Direction:

For the custard:

1. Put half of the milk on the fire with the vanilla sprig, another cinnamon stick, and the lemon skin, it should not boil.
2. In a bowl, add the cornstarch and sugar. Add the yolks and the rest of the milk and beat well with the hand or electric rod.
3. When the milk is very hot remove the cinnamon, vanilla, and lemon peel.
4. Add the yolk mixture and simmer while stirring until it thickens.
5. Once the right consistency is obtained, remove from heat. Stir and let cool to room temperature.
6. Prevent a dry layer from forming on top cover with paper towels. When it is cold, leave in the refrigerator until ready to use.

For the cake:

7. Spread the puff pastry.

8. Pour the cream over the puff pastry.

9. Then peel the apples, remove the heart and fillet. Sprinkle with a little lemon so that they do not darken.

10. Place on the custard one on top of the other.

11. Heat the air fryer a few minutes to 180^0C. If the whole mass does not fit in the air fryer, divide into two parts.

12. Put in the basket of the air fryer and set the timer of the air fryer about 10 or 15 minutes, then take out.

13. Sprinkle with sugar on top (2 tablespoons or so) and put back in the air fryer 10 minutes more, until the apple is soft. It will depend on the thickness of the apples. If they are cut thick, they will need more time.

14. If the sugar has not been caramelized, put the air fryer back on and gratin, taking care not to burn it.

15. Apart, place the syrup on the fire and add the jam, let it boil so that it mixes well and thickens a little, then reserve and strain.

16. Once the cake has cooled, cover the entire surface with the syrup and jam mixture, so that it has a shine. Let cool.

Nutrition Value (Nutrition per Serving):

- Calories: 259
- Fat: 13.08g
- Carbohydrate: 33.6g
- Protein: 2.48g
- Sugar: 14.45g
- Cholesterol: 0mg

Biscuits

Preparation time: 5 minutes. Cooking time: 8 minutes. Serve: 2

Ingredients:

- ¾ coconut sugar
- ¼ olive oil
- 1 egg
- ½ oat milk
- 1 sachet of yeast
- Oatmeal and brown rice flour (as needed)
- Cinnamon, orange zest, ginger, and vanilla (to taste)

Direction:

1. Gradually mix all the ingredients until they are integrated except the flours
2. Go putting the flour little by little and kneading until you get manageable dough and it does not stick. Be careful that it is not very dry since we work with flours that do not provide sponginess to the dough
3. You can use only oatmeal or mix them to taste
4. Once you have the dough, it only remains to make donuts or cookies as you prefer.
5. Place them in the air fryer at 200^0C for 7-8 minutes.

Nutrition Value (Nutrition per Serving):

- Calories: 81
- Fat: 4.1g
- Carbohydrates: 9.1g
- Protein: 1.1g
- Sugar: 1.2g
- Cholesterol: 0mg

Chocolate Cake

Preparation time: 15-20 minutes. Cooking time: 55 minutes. Serve: 4-6

Ingredients:

- 6 medium eggs
- 2 cups white sugar
- 250g of wheat flour
- Baking powder
- Cocoa powder

Direction:

1. Separate the egg whites from the egg yolks. Cream the egg whites with the help of a whisk. Increase the force until reaching snow points as the mixture firms. Beat the egg yolks and see incorporating the snow dots into this mixture.

2. Beat hard until the whites are integrated into the yolks. Then start adding the sugar little by little, cream until the lumps of the sugar dissolve well. At this point, it is your choice to season with a little vanilla or almond liqueur to lower the taste of the egg a little.

3. In another bowl, sift the wheat flour with the yeast and integrate it into the egg mixture little by little to beat it well and achieve a homogeneous texture. Finally, mix the cocoa. You can do it in two ways: 1) after pouring a first portion in the pan of the fryer without oil, 2) in the whole mixture and make or combined or chocolate completely.

4. Apart cut the cookie paper to the size of the oil-free fryer container. The paper can be smeared with butter on the side that is placed on the edges of the tray and does not have contact with the cake mixture and ensure that do not stick.

5. Start pouring the cake mixture into the air fryer that was preheated for 3 minutes, place the bowl, and set it to cook in 50 minutes at 140^0C. You can check the cooking every 10 minutes to verify that it is browning well and cooking the mixture.

Nutrition Value (Nutrition per Serving):

- Calories: 68
- Fat: 3g
- Carbohydrates: 7g
- Protein: 1g
- Sugar: 4g
- Cholesterol: 18mg

Gluten-Free Yogurt Cake

Preparation time: 5 minutes. Cooking time: 40 minutes. Serve: 2

Ingredients:

- 1 Greek yogurt
- 3 eggs
- 150g sugar
- 100g cream
- 50g sunflower oil
- 50g butter
- 200g gluten-free flour
- Pinch of salt
- 1 spoon yeast

Direction:

1. Put the eggs, yogurt, and sugar in the Thermomix, and mix well. Add the rest of the ingredients and mixtures.
2. Put the dough in the sponge cake container, previously brushed with oil. Preheat the fryer and put the mold with the dough for 40 minutes at 170^0C.
3. When cool, unmold and decorate to taste.

Nutrition Value (Nutrition per Serving):

- Calories: 361.47
- Proteins: 3.50g
- Carbohydrates: 50.29g
- Fat: 16.02g
- Sugar: 150g
- Cholesterol: 43mg

Conclusion

Throughout our trip in this eBook, you have seen many benefits of cooking and using an air fryer.

In the first chapter, we saw the basics of air fryers and an introduction into them, and in the other chapters many recipes as listed below:

- Chapter 2, 28 Snacks and Appetizers recipes
- Chapter 3, 28 Breakfast Recipes
- Chapter 4, 28 Poultry recipes
- Chapter 5, 29 Beef, Pork, Lamb Recipes
- Chapter 6, 33 Seafood and Fish recipes
- Chapter 7, 28 Vegan and Vegetarian Recipes and
- Chapter 8, 27 Desserts recipes

Remember, the processes of preparing recipes may vary if you have knowledge in cooking. If the proportions of the ingredients provided are respected, you will find the best flavors for your recipes, and your journey into using an air fryer will drastically cut down on the unhealthy, fried foods.

With the air fryer, you will discover a different flavor, but it's very similar to what you already know. The only real difference the air fryer makes is the amount of fat in your food. Invest in an air fryer and take the time to prolong your life by becoming a healthier version of yourself.

CPSIA information can be obtained
at www.ICGtesting.com
Printed in the USA
LVHW060207041120
670665LV00009B/17